SACRED OR SYNCRETIZED?

The Origins, Development, and Discernment of
Controversial Christian Observances

Dr. Antonio M. Palmer, D.Div

SACRED OR SYNCRETIZED?
The Origins, Development, and Discernment of Controversial Christian Observances

Published by:

Kingdom Publishing, 1350 Blair Drive, Suite F, Odenton, MD 21113

Printed in the United States of America

ISBN: 978-1-967006-14-4 (Paperback)
ISBN: 978-1-967006-15-1 (Ebook)

Supplementary Translations (Occasional Reference or Paraphrase)

- English Standard Version (ESV) – for clarity in theological discussion
- New International Version (NIV) – for accessibility in pastoral illustration

In some cases, Scripture was paraphrased or summarized for teaching purposes rather than quoted verbatim. Such paraphrases do not require copyright permission.

Dedication

To all Messianic followers—
who love the Scriptures, honor the Hebrew roots of the faith,
and seek to follow Jesus the Messiah with truth, humility, and
courage.
May this work serve unity, deepen understanding,
and keep Christ at the center of our shared hope.

ACKNOWLEDGMENTS

I would like to express my deepest gratitude to my wife, Dr. Barbara Palmer, whose wisdom, patience, and unwavering support sustained me throughout the writing of this work. I am also profoundly thankful for my church and Alliance family, whose love, prayers, and honest conversations continually sharpen my faith and calling.

Special thanks are extended to Dr. Leon Crawford, who consistently shared his thoughtful perspectives on various Christian observances and the reasons he follows them. Our dialogues were instrumental in shaping the balance and integrity of this study. I am equally grateful to my Messianic Israelite brothers, who openly shared their values, convictions, and lived experiences regarding these observances.

It is precisely because of the diversity of views—and my genuine love for both the Israelite and Gentile communities—that I felt compelled to write this work with clarity, fairness, and humility. Above all, I give thanks to God for salvation through the Messiah and for friends of *the Way* who continue to challenge us to seek truth with sincerity, grace, and courage.

TABLE OF CONTENTS

FOREWORD

The Christian faith is rooted in a historical revelation: God entered time and space in the person of Jesus Christ. From the beginning, followers of Christ have remembered, proclaimed, and embodied that revelation through preaching, worship, communal life, and sacred memory. Over time, however, the ways Christians have marked time, commemorated events, and structured devotion have developed in conversation with culture, empire, philosophy, and tradition. This book enters that long conversation with clarity, courage, and pastoral sobriety.

Few topics generate as much passion—and as much confusion— as the origins of Christian observances such as Christmas, Easter, Sunday worship, Lent, and All Saints' Day. In many churches today, these practices are embraced uncritically as sacred tradition; in others, they are rejected wholesale as pagan corruption. Still others occupy a middle ground, sensing that the truth lies somewhere between unthinking acceptance and reactionary dismissal. What has often been missing from the conversation is careful historical work combined with theological discernment and spiritual maturity.

This book does not set out to sensationalize Christian history, nor does it aim to dismantle the faith of sincere believers who observe these days with devotion to Christ. Rather, it seeks to do something far more difficult and far more necessary: to tell the truth. That truth includes acknowledging the Judaic foundations of early Christianity, the gradual separation between synagogue and church, the influence of the Roman world on Christian practice, and the complex process by which the church remembered Christ in a changing cultural landscape. It also includes recognizing where claims of "pagan origins" are historically grounded, where they are overstated, and where they are simply incorrect.

Equally important, this work asks a pastoral question that history alone cannot answer: How should faithful Christ followers live today in light of what we now know? The New Testament does not give believers a liturgical calendar, nor does it mandate annual holy days beyond the gospel proclamation itself. Yet it does call believers to worship in spirit and truth, to avoid idolatry in all its forms, and to walk in love, humility, and liberty of conscience. Holding these truths together requires wisdom rather than slogans, discernment rather than fear.

The strength of this book lies in its method. Each chapter engages primary historical sources, respected theologians, and recognized historians across Christian traditions. Assertions are documented, debates are fairly represented, and conclusions are drawn with care. Readers will find neither polemical attacks nor apologetic evasions, but a sustained effort to let evidence speak while Scripture remains the final authority for faith and practice.

At a time when Christianity is often divided between rigid traditionalism and rootless innovation, this book offers a third way: historically informed faithfulness. It invites readers to examine what they practice, why they practice it, and whether those practices point clearly to Christ or have become obscured by ritual, commercialism, or cultural habit. It challenges leaders to teach rather than assume, and believers to discern rather than merely inherit.

Whether one ultimately observes these Christian days, reinterprets them, or refrains from them altogether, the central question remains unchanged: Does Christ remain preeminent? If this book helps readers answer that question with greater integrity, humility, and understanding, it will have served the church well.

— Bishop Frank L. Holloman
Kingdom Celebration Center–Hampton Roads
Hampton, VA

PREFACE

This book was born out of a pastoral burden rather than a polemical agenda. For many years, I have listened to sincere believers wrestle with questions about Christian observances—questions often sparked by personal study, exposure to online debates, or encounters with traditions different from their own. Some approach these matters with unease, wondering whether practices they have cherished since childhood are biblically sound. Others respond with certainty, convinced that any observance not explicitly commanded in Scripture must be rejected outright. Between these two positions stands a large and often silent group of believers who simply want to honor Christ faithfully but are unsure how to navigate history, tradition, and conscience.

The purpose of this book is not to dictate practice but to cultivate discernment. Christianity is a historical faith, yet it is also a revealed faith. It emerged within Hebrew worship patterns, expanded across the Greco-Roman world, and endured through centuries of cultural, political, and theological change. In that process, the church adopted calendars, commemorations, and rituals that were never formally prescribed by Jesus or the apostles. Some of these developments were pastoral and edifying; others were shaped by imperial influence, theological controversy, or cultural accommodation. To pretend otherwise is to misunderstand the nature of church history.

At the same time, it would be historically and theologically irresponsible to label all post-biblical observances as "pagan" in a simplistic or sensational way. The early church did not merely absorb surrounding culture; it often redefined, reoriented, and contested it. Christian leaders wrestled with how to proclaim Christ in a world saturated with religious symbolism, seasonal festivals, and philosophical traditions. The results were not always uniform, nor were they always wise, but they were rarely accidental.

This book, therefore, seeks to slow the conversation down. Each chapter examines a specific observance—Christmas, Easter, Sunday worship, Lent, and All Saints' Day—by tracing its development from the earliest Christian communities through major historical milestones. Rather than beginning with modern assumptions, the analysis starts with Scripture, moves through the early church, and then follows the observable historical record. Claims are tested against evidence. Popular narratives are weighed against scholarly research. Where historians disagree, those disagreements are acknowledged rather than ignored.

A central concern of this work is the spiritual formation of believers today. History is not merely an academic exercise; it shapes how faith is practiced. Ritual can deepen devotion, but it can also replace it. Tradition can preserve truth, but it can also obscure it. Cultural familiarity can create comfort, but it can also dull discernment. For these reasons, each chapter does more than recount origins—it asks what elements of these observances may distract from Christ, foster ritualism, encourage commercialism, or blur the line between remembrance and reverence.

This book is written primarily for pastors, teachers, and serious students of Scripture, but it is not limited to the academy. Technical language is explained. Historical terms are defined. The goal is clarity rather than intimidation. Throughout, Scripture remains the final authority, even as the insights of historians and theologians help illuminate how the church arrived at its present practices.

I write as one who loves the church, respects its history, and believes deeply in the sufficiency of Christ. My hope is that this work will not create division, but maturity; not suspicion, but wisdom; not fear, but freedom. If it leads readers to examine their practices honestly, honor one another's conscience graciously, and keep Christ at the center of all remembrance, then it will have fulfilled its purpose.

— Bishop Dr. Antonio M. Palmer, D.Div

Introduction

WHY ORIGINS MATTER: SCRIPTURE, TRADITION, CULTURE, AND CONSCIENCE

Christianity proclaims a gospel rooted in history yet revealed by God. The incarnation, crucifixion, and resurrection of Jesus Christ occurred at identifiable moments in time, within a particular cultural and religious world. From the beginning, followers of Christ were compelled not only to believe these events but to remember them, proclaim them, and order their lives around them. Over centuries, this impulse to remember gave rise to calendars, observances, and rituals that now feel inseparable from Christian life. Yet familiarity does not always equal faithfulness, and tradition does not automatically confer biblical authority.

Questions surrounding the origins of Christmas, Easter, Sunday worship, Lent, and All Saints' Day are not new. They have surfaced repeatedly throughout church history—during the Reformation, among Puritans and Anabaptists, in revivalist movements. and more recently within Messianic, restorationist, and Hebraic-root communities. What is new is the speed and intensity with which claims circulate today. Assertions of "pagan origins" are often made without historical nuance, while defenses of tradition are sometimes offered without serious engagement with evidence. In this climate, believers are left either confused or polarized.

This book begins with a simple but necessary premise: origins matter, but they must be understood accurately. To ask where a practice came from is not to accuse it of corruption, nor is it to demand its abandonment. It is to seek truth. Scripture itself models this impulse, repeatedly calling God's people to remember, to examine their ways, and to test what they practice against divine revelation.

Sacred or Syncretized?

The apostolic writings do not provide a detailed liturgical calendar, but they do provide theological boundaries—warnings against idolatry, exhortations to liberty of conscience, and a persistent call to keep Christ central.

At the same time, Christianity did not develop in a vacuum. The early church existed within the Jewish world of feasts and Sabbaths and the Greco-Roman world of civic festivals, imperial ideology, and religious pluralism. As Christianity expanded beyond its Jewish roots, it faced practical questions: How should believers mark sacred time? How should Christ be proclaimed in societies already shaped by seasonal rituals and religious symbolism? How does one distinguish between adaptation for mission and accommodation that compromises faith? The answers given were not uniform, nor were they always free from political or cultural pressure.

The observances examined in this book emerged gradually, often centuries after the apostolic age. Christmas was not celebrated by the earliest Christians. Easter developed alongside debates about Passover and resurrection timing. Sunday worship took shape amid theological reflection and imperial legislation. Lent evolved through ascetic practices and penitential theology. All Saints' Day arose from the church's reverence for martyrs and its evolving understanding of death, memory, and intercession. None of these developments can be understood apart from history, yet none can be evaluated rightly apart from Scripture.

A key concern addressed throughout this work is the frequent claim that these observances are fundamentally pagan. While it is historically undeniable that Christianity encountered and sometimes repurposed elements of surrounding cultures, the word paganism is often used imprecisely. In some cases, similarities are superficial rather than genetic. In others, dates or symbols were intentionally reoriented toward Christian meaning. In still other cases, practices did absorb non-biblical elements that deserve careful scrutiny. This book refuses both extremes: it neither denies cultural influence nor reduces Christian history to syncretism.

Equally important is the pastoral question that follows historical inquiry: What should faithful Christ followers avoid? The New Testament consistently warns against practices that replace devotion to Christ with ritual, that substitute tradition for obedience, or that obscure the gospel beneath layers of cultural excess. It also warns against judgmentalism, legalism, and the elevation of human conscience to universal law. Faithfulness, therefore, requires more than historical knowledge; it requires wisdom, humility, and love.

This book is written with that balance in mind. It does not seek to tell every believer what they must observe or abandon. Instead, it seeks to equip readers with the tools to discern wisely—distinguishing remembrance from ritualism, symbolism from idolatry, liberty from license. Throughout, Scripture remains the final authority, while history serves as an honest witness to how the church has lived out its faith across time.

The chapters that follow will examine each observance carefully, drawing from Scripture, early Christian writings, church councils, reform movements, and modern scholarship. Claims will be documented. Myths will be challenged. Legitimate concerns will be taken seriously. Above all, the central question will remain constant: Do these practices glorify Christ, or do they risk obscuring Him?

Only by asking that question honestly can the church hold history and holiness together—and walk forward with both conviction and grace.

PART I

FOUNDATIONS FOR DISCERNMENT

Chapter 1

SCRIPTURE, TRADITION, AND THE DEVELOPMENT OF CHRISTIAN PRACTICE

Introduction: The Question Beneath the Observances

Before examining Christmas, Easter, Sunday worship, Lent, or All Saints' Day individually, a more foundational question must be addressed: How do Christian practices develop at all? The New Testament offers a clear proclamation of Christ but provides relatively little instruction concerning annual observances, liturgical calendars, or commemorative holy days. Yet by the fourth century, Christians across the Roman world were marking sacred time through feasts, fasts, and festivals that had become both devotional and institutional. Understanding how this transition occurred—and how it should be evaluated—requires a careful examination of Scripture, tradition, and historical development.

This chapter establishes the theological and historical framework for the entire book. It asks how authority functions within Christianity, how the early church navigated worship and memory, and how cultural forces shaped Christian practice over time. Without this foundation, discussions of "pagan influence" or "biblical legitimacy" quickly devolve into slogans rather than scholarship.

Scripture as the Final Authority in Christian Faith and Practice

The New Testament presents Scripture as the normative authority for doctrine and life. Jesus Himself appealed repeatedly to the written Word, rebuking religious leaders not for having traditions, but for allowing tradition to override divine command (Mark 7:6–13). The apostle Paul affirmed the formative role of Scripture in shaping belief and conduct, declaring it "profitable for teaching, for reproof, for correction, and for training in righteousness" (2 Timothy 3:16–17).

Yet Scripture does not function as a comprehensive manual for every aspect of Christian life. It gives principles rather than exhaustive regulations, especially concerning worship structures and sacred time. The earliest Christians gathered regularly, broke bread, prayed, and devoted themselves to apostolic teaching (Acts 2:42), but the New Testament does not prescribe a church calendar or annual holy days. This silence is itself instructive.

The apostolic writings reflect a tension between continuity with Hebrew worship patterns and freedom from Mosaic obligation. Judaic believers continued to observe feasts and Sabbaths, while Gentile believers were explicitly freed from such requirements (Acts 15:1–29). Paul warned against elevating days, seasons, or rituals as necessary for salvation, writing, "Let no one pass judgment on you in questions of food and drink, or with regard to a festival or a new moon or a Sabbath" (Colossians 2:16).[1]

This does not imply hostility toward remembrance or structured worship, but it does establish a boundary: no observance may be made salvific or compulsory. Any later Christian practice must therefore be evaluated not by its antiquity or popularity, but by its fidelity to the gospel and its consistency with apostolic teaching.

The Apostolic and Sub-Apostolic Church: Worship Without a Calendar

The first generations of Christians lived without formalized holy days. Early Christian writings from the first and second centuries emphasize ethical transformation, communal worship, and faithfulness under persecution rather than liturgical cycles. Scholars widely agree that *birthdays* were generally viewed with suspicion, often associated with pagan rulers and astrology rather than biblical faith.[2]

The earliest Christian focus was not on annual observances but on weekly gatherings centered on Scripture, prayer, and the Lord's Supper. Even then, the form of these gatherings varied widely by location. The Didache, one of the earliest Christian instructional texts, mentions fasting and prayer rhythms but does not prescribe annual festivals tied to Christ's life.[3]

What emerges from the historical record is a church that remembered Christ primarily through proclamation and participation, not commemoration. The gospel itself functioned as the central act of remembrance. As historian Larry Hurtado notes, early Christian devotion was "remarkably focused on Christ Himself rather than on ritual reenactment of sacred events."[4]

This early simplicity challenges modern assumptions. If Christianity could flourish for centuries without Christmas, Easter as we know it, or Lent, then these observances cannot be essential to the faith. At the same time, their later emergence does not automatically render them illegitimate. The question is not whether they existed in the apostolic era, but why and how they developed later.

Tradition: Transmission, Development, and Authority

Tradition, properly understood, is not the enemy of Scripture. The New Testament itself speaks positively of tradition *(paradosis)* when it refers to apostolic teaching faithfully transmitted (2 Thessalonians 2:15). Problems arise when tradition is detached from its apostolic anchor or elevated to unquestionable authority.

By the second and third centuries, Christian leaders increasingly appealed to tradition as a means of preserving orthodoxy against heresy. This was especially true in response to Gnosticism, which claimed secret knowledge apart from apostolic witness. Church fathers such as Irenaeus argued that true doctrine could be traced through the succession of bishops and the consistent teaching of the churches.[5]

While this emphasis helped protect core Christian beliefs, it also introduced a shift: authority began to move from Scripture alone toward Scripture as interpreted by ecclesial structures. Over time, practices developed within these structures gained a sense of sacred inevitability, even when their biblical basis was minimal or absent.

Theologian Jaroslav Pelikan famously observed that "tradition is the living faith of the dead; traditionalism is the dead faith of the living."[6] This distinction is crucial. Tradition can serve faith, but it can also fossilize it. When later observances are defended solely on the basis of longevity or institutional endorsement, they risk becoming forms of traditionalism rather than expressions of living faith.

The Role of Memory in Christian Worship

Christianity is a faith of remembrance. Jesus commanded His followers to remember Him through the breaking of bread and the sharing of the cup (Luke 22:19). The problem arises when remembrance shifts from participatory obedience to ritualized reenactment disconnected from daily discipleship.

As the church grew numerically and geographically, collective memory required structure. Martyr commemorations emerged as local communities honored those who had died for the faith. These were not initially celebrations of death, but affirmations of hope in resurrection.[7] Over time, such commemorations expanded, becoming more formal and calendrical.

Historians note that memory in ancient societies was not neutral; it shaped identity.[8] By marking time around sacred events, communities reinforced shared beliefs and boundaries. Christianity was no exception. As believers sought to catechize converts and resist pagan narratives, sacred time became a pedagogical tool.

This helps explain why observances developed even without explicit biblical mandates. They were attempts—sometimes sincere, sometimes flawed—to teach theology through time. The danger lay not in remembering Christ, but in confusing symbolic pedagogy with divine command.

Cultural Context: The Way, Greco-Roman Society, and Conversion

Early Christianity (The Way) existed at the crossroads of Judaic monotheism and Greco-Roman religious pluralism. Judaic worship was already structured around a calendar of feasts commemorating God's redemptive acts. Roman society, by contrast, was saturated with festivals honoring gods, emperors, and seasonal cycles.

As Gentiles entered the church in large numbers, Christian leaders faced practical challenges. Converts were accustomed to marking time religiously. A faith without sacred seasons may have seemed incomplete or unintelligible. Rather than abolish all notions of sacred time, Christian leaders often reoriented them.

This process, sometimes described as "Christianization," was complex. In some cases, dates were chosen to counter pagan festivals; in others, symbolism was deliberately subverted. Historian Ramsay MacMullen notes that the Christianization of the Roman world involved "adaptation as much as confrontation."[9]

This historical reality does not automatically imply compromise, but it does complicate simplistic narratives. The church neither absorbed paganism wholesale nor remained culturally untouched. It navigated a middle path, sometimes wisely, sometimes questionably.

When Adaptation Becomes Accommodation

Adaptation becomes accommodation when cultural forms reshape theology rather than serve it. This danger increased dramatically after Christianity gained imperial favor in the fourth century. Once Christianity moved from a marginal movement to a state-supported religion, political considerations influenced worship practices.

Sacred days provided a means of unifying populations, reinforcing imperial stability, and distinguishing Christian identity from rival religions. Theologian Peter Brown has shown how the cult of saints, feast days, and holy places functioned socially as well as spiritually.[10]

At this stage, observances began to carry institutional weight. Participation became expected. Non-participation could signal dissent. What began as voluntary remembrance risked becoming obligatory religion.

The Reformers later identified this shift as a core problem. Martin Luther did not reject all tradition but insisted that practices lacking scriptural warrant must not bind conscience. John Calvin argued that human-devised ceremonies, when imposed, "corrupt the pure worship of God."[11]

Their critiques remain relevant. The danger is not remembrance itself, but coercive remembrance—when believers are pressured to conform to practices that Scripture leaves to conscience.

Biblical Principles for Evaluating Christian Observances

From this historical and theological overview, several evaluative principles emerge:

1. Scripture is supreme: No observance may override or contradict biblical teaching.
2. Salvation is not mediated by ritual: Practices must never be treated as spiritually necessary.
3. Conscience must be respected: Believers may differ without judgment (Romans 14).
4. Christ must remain central: Any practice that obscures Christ's sufficiency is suspect.
5. History must be handled honestly: Neither romanticized nor demonized.

These principles will guide the chapters that follow. They allow for critical examination without cynicism and discernment without fear.

Conclusion: Setting the Stage for Discernment

This chapter has shown that Christian observances did not fall from heaven fully formed, nor were they uniformly imposed through conspiracy or corruption. They developed through a complex interplay of Scripture, tradition, memory, culture, and power. Some developments reflected pastoral wisdom; others reflected institutional convenience.

Understanding this process does not weaken faith—it strengthens it. When believers know why they practice what they practice, they are better equipped to worship in truth, avoid idolatry, and extend grace to those who differ. The chapters that follow will apply this framework to specific observances, beginning with Christmas, tracing each practice from its earliest roots through its historical development, and asking the central question: Does this observance faithfully serve the gospel of Christ?

Footnotes

1. The Holy Bible, English Standard Version (Wheaton, IL: Crossway, 2016), Col. 2:16.
2. Origen, *Homilies on Leviticus,* in *Ante-Nicene Fathers,* vol. 4 (Peabody, MA: Hendrickson, 1994), 291.
3. *The Didache,* trans. Michael W. Holmes, in *The Apostolic Fathers* (Grand Rapids: Baker Academic, 2007).
4. Larry W. Hurtado, *Lord Jesus Christ: Devotion to Jesus in Earliest Christianity* (Grand Rapids: Eerdmans, 2003), 135.
5. Irenaeus, *Against Heresies,* 3.3.1, in *Ante-Nicene Fathers,* vol. 1.
6. Jaroslav Pelikan, *The Vindication of Tradition* (New Haven: Yale University Press, 1984), 65.
7. Candida Moss, *The Myth of Persecution* (New York: HarperOne, 2013), 154–160.
8. Jan Assmann, *Religion and Cultural Memory* (Stanford:

Stanford University Press, 2006), 37–45.

9. Ramsay MacMullen, *Christianizing the Roman Empire* (New Haven: Yale University Press, 1984), 23.

10. Peter Brown, *The Cult of the Saints* (Chicago: University of Chicago Press, 1981), 12–18.

11. John Calvin, *Institutes of the Christian Religion,* trans. Henry Beveridge (Peabody, MA: Hendrickson, 2008), 4.10.23.

PART II

CONTESTED OBSERVANCES EXAMINED HISTORICALLY

Chapter 2

CHRISTMAS: FROM THE NATIVITY TO DECEMBER 25

Introduction: Remembering the Birth of Christ

Few Christian observances evoke as much affection, controversy, and confusion as Christmas. For many believers, it is a season of joy centered on the incarnation of Jesus Christ—the eternal Word made flesh. For others, it represents a troubling blend of religious tradition, cultural excess, and practices allegedly borrowed from paganism. Still others observe it with ambivalence, unsure whether honoring Christ's birth on December 25 is biblically appropriate or historically defensible.

This chapter examines Christmas historically and theologically, asking three interrelated questions:

1. Did the earliest Christians celebrate the birth of Jesus?
2. How and why did December 25 emerge as the dominant date?
3. To what extent did non-Christian practices influence the celebration of Christmas, and how should faithful Christ followers respond?

Rather than beginning with modern debates, this chapter traces Christmas from its absence in the apostolic era through its gradual development in the fourth century and beyond. It distinguishes between commemoration and command, historical evidence and speculation, and cultural adaptation and theological compromise. Only then can the question of pagan influence be addressed responsibly.

The Absence of Christmas in the New Testament and Early Christianity

The New Testament records the birth of Jesus in detail, particularly in the Gospels of Matthew and Luke. Yet it is striking that no date is given, and no command is issued to commemorate the event annually. The apostolic preaching in Acts centers overwhelmingly on the death and resurrection of Christ, not His nativity. This emphasis reflects the theological heart of early Christian proclamation: salvation accomplished through the cross and confirmed by the resurrection.

Early Christian writers confirm this silence. The earliest generations of believers did not celebrate Jesus' birth as a festival. In fact, birthday celebrations were often viewed negatively in early Christian thought, associated more closely with pagan rulers and astrology than with biblical faith. Origen of Alexandria, writing in the third century, criticized birthday celebrations outright, noting that Scripture records the birthdays of Pharaoh and Herod—both figures associated with violence and oppression—but never those of the righteous.[1]

Modern historians widely agree that Christmas did not exist as a Christian feast during the first two centuries. Thomas J. Talley observes that "there is no evidence for the celebration of Christmas as a festival before the late third or early fourth century."[2] This absence is not accidental. Early Christianity was shaped by persecution, marginalization, and a strong expectation of Christ's return. The community's focus was ethical transformation and gospel proclamation, not liturgical expansion.

This historical reality establishes an important boundary: Christmas is not apostolic in origin. It is a later development, which must therefore be evaluated as a human tradition rather than a divine mandate.

Early Speculation About the Date of Jesus' Birth

Although early Christians did not celebrate Christmas, they were not indifferent to chronology. As theological reflection deepened, some writers began to speculate about the timing of Jesus' birth—not for liturgical reasons, but for symbolic and theological ones.

Clement of Alexandria, writing around the end of the second century, records that various groups proposed dates ranging from April to May, and even January.[3] Notably, Clement presents these calculations almost as curiosities, not as foundations for worship. They reflect an intellectual interest rather than a devotional practice.

One important theological assumption emerged during this period: the belief that great prophets died on the same calendar date as their conception. This idea, rooted in Jewish symbolic thinking, later played a crucial role in the selection of December 25. According to this logic, if Jesus was crucified on March 25 (a date many early Christians believed), then His conception would also have occurred on March 25—placing His birth nine months later, on December 25.[4]

This calculation theory, supported by scholars such as Louis Duchesne and Thomas Talley, suggests that December 25 arose from internal Christian symbolism, not from the adoption of a pagan festival.[5] This point is critical, as it directly challenges one of the most common modern claims about Christmas's origins.

The Emergence of December 25 in the Fourth Century

The first clear evidence of Christmas being celebrated on December 25 appears in the fourth century, after Christianity gained legal recognition under Constantine. The Chronography of 354, a Roman almanac, lists December 25 as the birth of Christ (natus Christus in Betleem Iudeae).[6]

This period marked a significant shift in Christian life. Persecution gave way to imperial patronage, and Christianity moved from the margins to the center of public life. As the church expanded rapidly, there was a growing need for structured teaching, standardized worship, and shared sacred time. Festivals served catechetical purposes, reinforcing doctrine among a largely illiterate population.

Christmas, in this context, functioned as a theological affirmation of the incarnation. In the face of lingering Christological controversies—particularly debates over the full divinity and humanity of Christ—the celebration of Jesus' birth in the flesh became doctrinally significant. Church leaders such as Athanasius emphasized the incarnation as essential to salvation, making a festival commemorating Christ's birth pastorally useful.[7]

Thus, Christmas did not arise in a vacuum. It emerged at a moment when theology, empire, and pedagogy intersected.

Saturnalia, Sol Invictus, and the Paganism Question

The most persistent criticism of Christmas is that December 25 was chosen to replace or absorb pagan festivals, particularly Saturnalia and the feast of Sol Invictus (the Unconquered Sun). These claims are often repeated without distinction, leading to confusion.

Saturnalia was a popular Roman festival held in mid-December, characterized by feasting, gift-giving, and social inversion. However, it typically occurred between December 17 and 23, not on December 25.[8] While cultural overlap is undeniable—winter festivity was common across cultures—there is little evidence that Christmas directly replaced Saturnalia.

The cult of Sol Invictus presents a more complex case. In 274 CE, Emperor Aurelian established December 25 as the feast day of the Unconquered Sun. Some scholars argue that Christians adopted this date to offer a rival celebration, proclaiming Christ as the true "Sun of Righteousness" (Malachi 4:2). Others argue the opposite—that pagan authorities selected December 25 in response to an already developing Christian tradition.[9]

What can be said with confidence is this: the historical evidence does not support a simplistic borrowing narrative. As historian Steven Hijmans cautions, "there is no clear evidence that the Christian feast of Christmas was deliberately set to coincide with pagan solar festivals."[10] The relationship between the two is one of chronological proximity, not proven causation.

Medieval Expansion and Cultural Layering

During the Middle Ages, Christmas expanded dramatically in scope and expression. Liturgical observances multiplied, nativity plays emerged, and popular customs developed alongside ecclesiastical rituals. This period introduced many elements now commonly associated with Christmas—but absent from its early history.

Practices such as evergreen decorations, Yule logs, and later Christmas trees have roots in Germanic and northern European winter symbolism. These customs were gradually Christianized as Europe converted to Christianity. Missionaries often tolerated or reinterpreted local traditions rather than attempting to erase them entirely.[11]

This process of cultural layering complicates the question of pagan influence. Some elements clearly originated outside Christianity, yet were later invested with Christian meaning. The problem arises when symbolism overshadows substance, or when cultural practices are assumed to be inherently sacred.

Reformation leaders responded differently to these developments. Martin Luther retained Christmas but emphasized preaching and Christ-centered devotion. Puritans, particularly in England and colonial America, rejected Christmas altogether, viewing it as an unbiblical invention corrupted by excess and superstition.[12] Their objections highlight a recurring tension: tradition versus biblical warrant.

Modern Christmas: Commercialization and Secularization

In the modern era, Christmas has undergone yet another transformation. Industrialization, consumer culture, and secular nationalism reshaped the holiday into a largely commercial event. Sociologists note that Christmas in the West often functions more as a cultural festival than a religious observance.[13]

This shift raises serious concerns for faithful Christ followers. Even if Christmas originated as a Christ-centered commemoration, its modern expression often marginalizes Christ altogether. The danger here is not paganism in the ancient sense, but idolatry of consumption, nostalgia, and sentimentality.

Theologian Stanley Hauerwas warns that when Christian festivals are absorbed into consumer culture, they cease to form Christian character and instead reinforce secular values.[14] Christmas becomes less about incarnation and more about indulgence.

Santa Claus, Flying Reindeer, Elves, and the Making of "Mythic Christmas"

A major source of confusion in Christian debates is that people argue about "Christmas" as if it were one thing. But much controversy is really about Santa-centered folklore and consumer practice, not about worshiping Christ.

So where did Santa Claus (as we know him) come from?

The Deep Root: St. Nicholas of Myra and Medieval Gift Traditions

Behind Santa stands a historical Christian figure: Nicholas of Myra (fourth-century bishop), revered for generosity in later Christian memory. Nicholas devotion and gift customs attached to his feast day (December 6 in the Western tradition, with calendar variations in other traditions). Popular stories about Nicholas—especially anonymous giving—helped form a durable "gift-bringer" archetype.[15]

During and after the Protestant Reformation, many Protestant communities resisted saint veneration, sometimes shifting gift customs away from St. Nicholas' day to Christmas. This is one reason why, in some cultures, gift-giving moved from early December into late December rhythms.

The key point: the earliest "Santa" stream is not pagan; it is Christian hagiographical memory around a bishop, filtered through medieval custom.

The American Reinvention: Dutch Sinterklaas and New York's "Knickerbocker" Santa

The *modern* Santa is not a simple continuation of medieval St. Nicholas. He is largely a nineteenth-century American cultural construction—a hybrid of St. Nicholas, Dutch-American Sinterklaas memory, English "Father Christmas" motifs, and later commercial art.

In early U.S. culture, writers helped reshape St. Nicholas into a local ethnic symbol. Washington Irving's A History of New York (1809), published under the persona "Diedrich Knickerbocker," is widely discussed as part of New York's cultural project to celebrate Dutch heritage; later New York institutions promoted St. Nicholas imagery as civic identity.[16] The New York Public Library's historical overview of Santa's New York roots highlights Irving's role in this early American reframing.[17]

This phase matters because it shows Santa's "center of gravity" shifting from church devotion to cultural storytelling.

The Breakthrough Text: "A Visit from St. Nicholas" and the Birth of Flying Reindeer

The single most influential Santa text in American history is the poem commonly known as "'Twas the Night Before Christmas"

("A Visit from St. Nicholas"), first published in 1823. The poem popularized a cluster of features that became standard:

- Santa arriving on Christmas Eve (not St. Nicholas Day)
- A sleigh with eight reindeer, each named
- Santa traveling through the sky and entering by chimney
- A jolly, plump, elf-like figure ("a right jolly old elf")

The poem is frequently credited with cementing "reindeer flight" as a core motif and re-centering St. Nicholas mythology on Christmas Eve domestic imagination.[18] The Poetry Foundation and Poets.org preserve the text and its interpretive framing as a foundational American cultural artifact.[19]

This is one of the clearest historical answers to your specific request: flying reindeer enter "mainstream Santa" through early nineteenth-century American literature, not through ancient pagan religion.

Thomas Nast: The North Pole, the Workshop, and the Rise of Elves

If Moore's poem built the narrative, illustrator Thomas Nast helped build the visual "world" of Santa. During the Civil War era and after, Nast published influential Santa images in Harper's Weekly, including portrayals that contributed to:

- Santa as a robust, fur-trimmed figure
- Santa's association with a toy workshop
- Santa's residence at (or linkage to) the North Pole
- The conceptual ecosystem that later supports elves as helpers

Smithsonian's historical treatment notes Nast's importance in cementing Santa's modern image in American imagination, beginning with Civil War-era illustrations.[20] Archival resources and institutional summaries connected to Nast's work emphasize the significance of these images for the "North Pole Santa" mythology.[21]

Here again, the lineage is not pagan religion but print culture—art, publishing, and nation-building.

Coca-Cola and the Standardization of Santa's Modern Look

A common modern claim is: "Coca-Cola invented Santa." The more accurate historical statement is: Coca-Cola did not invent Santa, but it helped standardize and globalize one particular Santa image through mass advertising.

Beginning in 1931, Coca-Cola commissioned illustrator Haddon Sundblom for Santa images that portrayed a warm, friendly, human-like Santa—an image that became widely reproduced. The Coca-Cola Company's own corporate history acknowledges the intentional design of a "wholesome" Santa and the long-running influence of Sundblom's campaign.[22] A university-hosted scholarly thesis on Coca-Cola's use of Sundblom's Santa further documents how the company later revived and leveraged these images as nostalgia marketing.[23]

So the red-suited, universally recognizable Santa is best understood as a mass-media product—a cultural icon shaped by advertising, not ecclesial tradition.

Rudolph (1939) and the "Ninth Reindeer" as Retail Folklore

The "original eight" reindeer are tied to Moore's 1823 poem. Rudolph is much later. He was created in 1939 as a promotional story for Montgomery Ward, written by copywriter Robert L. May. Smithsonian's National Museum of American History summarizes Rudolph's origin explicitly as a marketing giveaway and dates it to 1939.[24]

Rudolph's rise illustrates a broader point: the Santa ecosystem continues to expand through commercial creativity. New characters and lore are added not through church councils or devotional practice but through retail and entertainment pipelines.

Discernment: Paganism, Folklore, and What Faithful Christ Followers Should Avoid

Are Santa, Reindeer, and Elves "Pagan"? A Better Question

From a strict historical standpoint, most Santa-world elements (flying reindeer, North Pole workshop, named reindeer, elves as toy-makers, Rudolph) are better classified as <u>modern folklore</u> than pagan religion. Their roots are largely in:

- medieval saint memory (Nicholas traditions),
- early American ethnic-cultural storytelling (New York/ Dutch memory),
- nineteenth-century poetry and illustration (Moore, Nast),
- twentieth-century advertising and retail invention (Coca-Cola Santa; Montgomery Ward's Rudolph).

That does not mean everything is spiritually harmless. It means "pagan origins" is often the wrong diagnostic category. The more pressing issues are typically truth, discipleship, conscience, and cultural domination.

What Faithful Christ Followers Should Avoid Regarding Christmas (Expanded)

Here are biblically grounded caution zones—some apply whether one celebrates Christmas religiously or not:

A. <u>Avoid making Christmas a test of salvation or spirituality</u>
   Christmas may be observed or abstained from without condemning others (Rom. 14:5–6). Any practice that binds conscience beyond Scripture risks becoming a rival law (cf. Col. 2:16).

B. <u>Avoid letting cultural Christmas displace worship and obedience</u>

A believer can "honor Christ" with words while letting the season train the heart toward greed, envy, debt, or status performance. Schmidt's analysis of consumer holiday "rites" is useful precisely because it shows how market practices become formative rituals.[25]

C. <u>Avoid commercialization that eclipses Christ</u>
Nissenbaum's and Schmidt's work helps explain how *modern* Christmas became culturally "domesticated" and commercially intensified—often muting Christian meaning under gift economies and sentimentality.[26]

D. <u>Avoid deception and manipulation—especially with children</u>
This is not a call for one universal rule, but a warning: Christians must think carefully about truth-telling, discipleship, and the formation of trust. Some families treat Santa as playful storytelling; others treat him as literal omniscient judge ("naughty or nice"), which can unintentionally catechize children into moralism or confusion about divine attributes. Wisdom and conscience matter here.

E. <u>Avoid practices that flirt with occult themes or dark imagery</u>
Not everything "spooky" is inherently occult, but Christians should avoid normalizing fascination with darkness, fear, or spiritual impurity—especially when blended into a season meant to proclaim the Light of Christ.

F. <u>Avoid judging other believers</u>
Some believers can celebrate Christmas with deep Christ-centered devotion; others abstain from conscience and conviction. Scripture repeatedly warns against despising and condemning one another over disputable matters (Rom. 14).

Conclusion: Christmas as Doctrine, Christmas as Culture

Historically, Christmas as a Christian feast is a later development (especially visible from the fourth century onward), and the choice of December 25 cannot responsibly be reduced to a simplistic pagan-borrowing narrative. Culturally, however, modern Christmas has been massively reshaped by folklore, print culture, advertising, and consumer capitalism—especially through the evolution of Santa Claus and his expanding mythos.

For faithful Christ followers, the question is not only Where did Christmas come from? but also:

What is Christmas doing to us—spiritually, ethically, economically, and devotionally?

In the next chapter, we will examine Easter: its relationship to Passover, early Christian resurrection observance, the Quartodeciman controversy, and the later development of popular symbols and calendar calculations.

Footnotes

1. Origen, *Homilies on Leviticus,* in *Ante-Nicene Fathers,* vol. 4 (Peabody, MA: Hendrickson, 1994), 291.
2. Thomas J. Talley, *The Origins of the Liturgical Year* (Collegeville, MN: Liturgical Press, 1991), 88.
3. Clement of Alexandria, *Stromata* 1.21, in *Ante-Nicene Fathers,* vol. 2.
4. Augustine, *On the Trinity* 4.5, trans. Edmund Hill (Brooklyn: New City Press, 1991).
5. Louis Duchesne, *Christian Worship: Its Origin and Evolution* (London: SPCK, 1904), 260–262.
6. *Chronography of 354,* trans. Michele Renee Salzman (Oxford: Oxford University Press, 1990).
7. Athanasius, *On the Incarnation,* trans. John Behr (Yonkers, NY: St. Vladimir's Seminary Press, 2011).

8. H. H. Scullard, *Festivals and Ceremonies of the Roman Republic* (Ithaca: Cornell University Press, 1981), 206–210.

9. Steven Hijmans, "Sol Invictus, the Winter Solstice, and the Origins of Christmas," Mouseion 3, no. 3 (2003): 377–398.

10. Steven Hijmans, "Usener's Christmas," *Phoenix 57,* no. 3–4 (2003): 377.

11. Ronald Hutton, *The Stations of the Sun* (Oxford: Oxford University Press, 1996), 1–35.

12. Stephen Nissenbaum, *The Battle for Christmas* (New York: Knopf, 1996), 3–40.

13. Leigh Eric Schmidt, *Consumer Rites: The Buying and Selling of American Holidays* (Princeton: Princeton University Press, 1995), 187–210.

14. Stanley Hauerwas, *A Community of Character* (Notre Dame: University of Notre Dame Press, 1981), 45–47.

15. Gerry Bowler, *Santa Claus: A Biography* (Toronto: McClelland & Stewart, 2005).

16. Washington Irving, *A History of New York,* ed. (Project Gutenberg text of 1809 work) (December 1809).

17. "Santa's New York Roots," New York Public Library (Dec. 9, 2015).

18. Clement Clarke Moore (attrib.), "A Visit from St. Nicholas," first published Troy Sentinel (Dec. 23, 1823).

19. "A Visit from St. Nicholas," Poetry Foundation (accessed 2025).

20. "A Civil War Cartoonist Created the Modern Image of Santa Claus," *Smithsonian Magazine* (Dec. 19, 2018).

21. "Santa Claus and His Works," HarpWeek (Harper's Weekly archive) (accessed 2025).

22. "Haddon Sundblom and the Coca-Cola Santas," The Coca-Cola Company (accessed 2025).

23. A. Weatherford, "Things Go Better with Nostalgia: 'How the Coca-Cola Company Used Haddon Sundblom's Santa Claus Illustrations…'" (M.A. thesis, Middle Tennessee State University, 2019), PDF.
24. "Rudolph the Red-Nosed Reindeer," Smithsonian National Museum of American History (Dec. 21, 2010).
25. Schmidt, *Consumer Rites.*
26. Nissenbaum, *Battle for Christmas;* Schmidt, *Consumer Rites.*

Chapter 3

EASTER: RESURRECTION, PASSOVER, AND THE STRUGGLE FOR SACRED TIME

Introduction: The Heart of the Christian Proclamation

If Christmas proclaims the mystery of the incarnation, Easter announces the triumph of redemption. At the very center of Christian faith stands the resurrection of Jesus Christ—not as a peripheral doctrine or symbolic hope, but as the decisive act of God in history. The apostle Paul leaves no ambiguity: "If Christ has not been raised, your faith is futile and you are still in your sins" (1 Corinthians 15:17). From the earliest apostolic preaching to contemporary Christian confession, the resurrection functions as the axis upon which Christian theology, ethics, and hope turn.

Yet while the resurrection itself is apostolic, essential, and non-negotiable, the formal observance of Easter as an annual festival is a later historical development. Like Christmas, Easter raises critical questions regarding Scripture, tradition, calendar authority, and cultural adaptation. Unlike Christmas, however, Easter is inseparably tethered to biblical chronology, because the death and resurrection of Jesus occurred during Passover. This connection introduces complexities that shaped some of the earliest and most consequential debates in church history.

This chapter explores Easter by tracing the relationship between event and observance, between biblical revelation and historical development. It examines the resurrection proclamation in the New Testament, the Judaic roots of early Christian *Pascha,* the Quartodeciman controversy, the Council of Nicaea's calendrical decisions, recurring claims of pagan influence, and the pastoral implications for faithful Christ-followers today. Throughout, a guiding distinction remains clear: the resurrection is divinely revealed; Easter as a festival is historically developed.

Resurrection in the New Testament: Proclamation Before Celebration

The New Testament contains no command to observe an annual resurrection festival. What it does contain is relentless resurrection proclamation. The resurrection dominates apostolic preaching (Acts 2; 3; 4; 10; 13), shapes early Christian ethics (Romans 6), and anchors Christian hope (1 Corinthians 15; 1 Thessalonians 4). Resurrection is not treated as a commemorative memory but as an ongoing reality that defines Christian identity and existence.

The earliest Christian acts of remembrance were not annual festivals but weekly gatherings and sacramental participation, especially the Lord's Supper. Jesus explicitly commanded remembrance of His death—"Do this in remembrance of me" (Luke 22:19; 1 Corinthians 11:23–26)—but issued no command regarding an annual celebration of His resurrection. This does not diminish the resurrection's importance; rather, it clarifies how memory functioned in apostolic Christianity. Christ's death was ritually remembered because it was not yet fully visible in the world; His resurrection was proclaimed because it inaugurated a new age.

New Testament scholars consistently note that early Christians lived in an eschatological posture, anticipating Christ's imminent return. Oscar Cullmann famously argued that early Christianity understood time not cyclically but redemptively. In Christ and Time, he demonstrates that the resurrection did not introduce a new sacred anniversary but reshaped time itself, inaugurating the "already/not yet" reality of the kingdom of God.[1] Resurrection faith therefore did not require an annual ritual to sustain its meaning.

Easter: Resurrection, Passover, and the Quartodeciman
Controversy

James D. G. Dunn further reinforces this point by situating resurrection belief firmly within Second Temple Judaic apocalyptic expectation, not pagan seasonal mythology. In The Partings of the Ways, Dunn demonstrates that early Christian resurrection theology flowed directly from Judaic hope rooted in Danielic eschatology and covenantal fulfillment—not from fertility symbolism or dying-and-rising god myths.[2] Resurrection proclamation preceded resurrection celebration because resurrection defined the entire Christian worldview.

This establishes an essential principle for the entire chapter: theological centrality does not automatically require liturgical formalization.

Passover and the Judaic Matrix of Resurrection Faith

Jesus was crucified during Passover (Matthew 26–27; Mark 14–15; Luke 22–23; John 18–19). This historical reality is not incidental. Passover commemorated Israel's deliverance from Egypt through the blood of the lamb (Exodus 12), and the New Testament explicitly presents Jesus as the fulfillment of this typology: "Christ, our Passover lamb, has been sacrificed" (1 Corinthians 5:7).

The earliest Christians—who were overwhelmingly Judaic—understood Jesus' death and resurrection within the Passover framework. Early Christian *Pascha* was not initially a separate Christian feast but a Christ-centered interpretation of Passover. Brant Pitre emphasizes that the Last Supper itself was a Passover meal, making the death and resurrection of Jesus inseparable from Israel's liturgical calendar.[3] The resurrection was understood not as a rupture from Israel's story, but as its climax.

This is why early resurrection remembrance was often tied to Nisan 14, the Passover date in the Hebrew calendar, regardless of the day of the week. This practice reflected fidelity to biblical chronology and apostolic memory rather than innovation. David Instone-

Brewer's research into Hebrew calendar disputes demonstrates that such disagreements were common within "Judaism" itself, further contextualizing early Christian debates as intra-biblical rather than apostate departures.[4]

This Passover-rooted understanding shaped early Christian theology long before it shaped liturgical calendars. Easter controversies did not arise from pagan pressure but from questions of how best to honor the biblical timeline of redemption.

The Quartodeciman Controversy: Date Before Doctrine

One of the earliest recorded disputes in church history concerned when to observe Christ's death and resurrection. Known as the Quartodeciman controversy (from the Latin quartodecimus, "fourteenth"), this conflict revolved around whether Christians should commemorate Christ's passion on Nisan 14 or on the Sunday following Passover.

Christians in Asia Minor, claiming apostolic authority through figures such as the apostle John and Polycarp, observed Christ's death on Nisan 14 regardless of the weekday. Christians in Rome and elsewhere insisted that the resurrection must be celebrated on Sunday, the day Christ rose. Importantly, this was not initially a divisive dispute.

Eusebius records that Polycarp traveled to Rome to discuss the matter with Bishop Anicetus in the mid-second century. They acknowledged disagreement yet maintained fellowship, demonstrating that early Christianity allowed diversity of practice without doctrinal condemnation.[1] By the late second century, however, Bishop Victor of Rome attempted to enforce uniformity, threatening excommunication. Irenaeus rebuked this effort, appealing to earlier tolerance and warning against fracturing the church over non-essential matters.[2]

Easter: Resurrection, Passover, and the Quartodeciman Controversy

Paul F. Bradshaw argues that this diversity reflects localized fidelity to apostolic memory rather than theological confusion. Uniformity, he notes, emerged later due to ecclesial consolidation rather than doctrinal necessity.[5] Andrew McGowan similarly observes that early Christian worship was relational and communal, not rigidly calendrical.[6]

The Quartodeciman controversy reveals a crucial point: early Easter debates were intra-Christian and calendar-based, not pagan-driven.

From Diversity to Uniformity: The Council of Nicaea

The question of Easter dating was ultimately addressed at the Council of Nicaea (325 CE). While best known for addressing Christological doctrine, the council also sought to establish a unified method for determining Easter. It decreed that Easter should be celebrated on the same Sunday throughout the Christian world, calculated independently of the Hebrew calendar.

Constantine's surviving correspondence reveals that this decision was motivated not only by theological concerns but also by political and cultural considerations. His language reflects anti-Judah sentiment, emphasizing that Christians should not follow "the customs of the Jews." Ramsay MacMullen demonstrates that Constantine's religious policies were shaped by imperial pragmatism; uniform Easter observance served imperial unity as much as ecclesial clarity.[7]

Peter Leithart critiques this post-Nicene reliance on imperial power, warning that state regulation subtly reshaped Christian identity from a countercultural community into a civic religion.[8] Easter became a church-controlled calendrical event, even as its biblical foundation remained intact.

The Name "Easter" and the Paganism Debate

One of the most persistent claims is that Easter is named after a pagan goddess—often identified as Eostre or Ishtar. Historically, this claim collapses under scrutiny. The only ancient source linking Eostre to a deity is the eighth-century monk Bede, who mentions a spring month named after a goddess. No archaeological or liturgical evidence supports widespread worship of such a figure.

Moreover, the term Easter appears only in English and some Germanic languages. In most Christian languages, the feast is called *Pascha,* directly derived from *Pesach* (Passover). Ronald Hutton argues that while spring symbolism is widespread, there is insufficient evidence to assert pagan derivation. J. N. D. Kelly likewise warns against retrojecting later folklore into early doctrine.[9]

N. T. Wright's exhaustive work demonstrates that Christian resurrection theology is fundamentally distinct from pagan dying-and-rising god myths, which lacked bodily resurrection and covenantal fulfillment.[10] Parallel symbolism does not equal origin.

Eggs, Rabbits, and Spring Imagery

Popular Easter imagery—eggs, rabbits, flowers—entered Christian practice centuries later, primarily through folk culture. Eggs often symbolized life and were associated with the end of Lenten fasting. Rabbits entered Easter symbolism in German folklore. These are cultural accretions, not theological foundations.

The danger lies not in symbols themselves but in allowing them to displace resurrection proclamation.

Easter in the Reformation and Modern Church

Reformation leaders diverged in their approach. Martin Luther retained Easter preaching but rejected compulsory observance.[11] John Calvin permitted Easter but warned against superstition and conscience-binding ceremonies.[12] Radical reformers rejected Easter altogether.

In the modern era, Easter often becomes a cultural spectacle. Michael Horton critiques contemporary Easter practice for substituting spectacle for catechesis, while Wright warns that metaphorical resurrection empties Easter of its historical power.[13]

What Faithful Christ Followers Should Avoid Regarding Easter

Faithful believers should therefore:

1. Avoid detaching resurrection from discipleship (Romans 6)
2. Avoid elevating Easter to salvific requirement (Galatians 4:9–11)
3. Avoid anti-Judah rhetoric
4. Avoid symbolic clutter that obscures the gospel
5. Avoid judging fellow believers (Romans 14)

Conclusion: Resurrection Without Rival

Easter, like Christmas, is a historical development layered onto a biblical event. The resurrection is non-negotiable; the festival is optional. When rightly understood, Easter proclaims victory. When misunderstood, it risks ritual without power.

Faithful Christ followers are called not merely to celebrate Easter, but to live resurrection—daily, visibly, and uncompromisingly.

Comparative Table: Passover, Easter (Pascha), and Pagan Spring Festivals

Category	Biblical Passover (Pesach)	Christian Easter	Pagan Spring Festivals
Historical Timing	Fixed by Judaic lunar calendar	Initially tied to Passover; later standardized to Sunday after full moon	Aligned with solstices, equinoxes, and farming seasons
Early Observance	Mandatory covenantal feast of Israel	Diverse early Christian practice (Quartodeciman vs. Sunday observance)	Civic and religious celebrations tied to local customs
Relationship to Resurrection	Typology (fulfilled in Christ according to NT)	Direct proclamation of resurrection	No bodily resurrection theology
Calendar Authority	Scripture-based, covenantally binding for Israel	Church-determined after Nicaea (325 CE)	Local priesthoods, rulers, or tradition
Language Usage	Pesach (Hebrew)	Pascha (Greek/Latin); "Easter" in some Germanic languages	Names vary widely by culture
Symbolism	Lamb, blood, unleavened bread	Cross, empty tomb, new creation	Eggs, animals, plants, seasonal fertility

Easter: Resurrection, Passover, and the Quartodeciman Controversy

Claimed Pagan Influence	None	Often alleged due to timing and later folk symbols	Indigenous to pagan religions
Scholarly Assessment	Biblically mandated and historically continuous	Biblically grounded event; festival historically developed	Theologically unrelated to Christian resurrection
Theological Focus	Deliverance and covenant faithfulness	Salvation, resurrection, eschatological hope	Cycles of nature, prosperity, continuity
Modern Confusion Point	Sometimes dismissed by Christians as "Jewish"	Often accused of paganism without evidence	Mistakenly treated as Easter's origin
Key Scholarly Consensus	Foundational to understanding Christ's death	Resurrection is essential; festival is optional	Parallels ≠ origins

Interpretive Summary (For Readers)

- Passover (Pesach) is a biblically commanded covenant feast with deep theological continuity into the New Testament
- Easter (Pascha) is a historically developed Christian observance centered on a non-negotiable biblical event (the resurrection), but not itself commanded as a festival.
- Pagan spring festivals are religiously and theologically distinct, even where symbolic or seasoal similarities exist.

Shared timing or symbols do not equal shared origin.
Historical method requires evidence of transmission—not mere resemblance.

Visual Timeline: From Passover to Pascha to Easter

c. 1300 BCE — Biblical Passover Instituted
Exodus 12
- God institutes Passover as a covenantal memorial of Israel's deliverance from Egypt
- Blood of the lamb, unleavened bread, and divine redemption
- Passover is commanded, recurring, and theologically foundational

Key Insight: Passover establishes a redemptive-time framework that later Christians interpret christologically.

c. 30–33 CE — Death and Resurrection of Jesus
Gospel Accounts
- Jesus is crucified during Passover
- Resurrection occurs on the first day of the week
- Jesus is proclaimed as the true Passover Lamb (1 Cor. 5:7)

Key Insight: The resurrection is an event, not yet a festival.

c. 30–100 CE — Apostolic Era
New Testament Period
- Resurrection proclaimed constantly (Acts, Epistles)
- No annual resurrection feast commanded
- Weekly gatherings and the Lord's Supper dominate remembrance

Key Insight: Early Christianity is proclamation-centered, not calendar-centered.

2nd Century (c. 100–190 CE) — Early Pascha Observance
Quartodeciman Practice
- Many Christians observe Christ's death/resurrection on Nisan 14

Easter: Resurrection, Passover, and the Quartodeciman Controversy

- Strong continuity with Jewish Passover chronology
- Diversity of practice without initial schism

Key Insight: The first "Easter" debates are about dating, not paganism.

Mid–Late 2nd Century — Quartodeciman Controversy
Asia Minor vs. Rome

- Disagreement: fixed Passover date vs. Sunday celebration
- Leaders like Polycarp and Anicetus maintain fellowship
- Victor of Rome later attempts enforcement, rebuked by peers

Key Insight: Unity existed despite calendrical disagreement.

325 CE — Council of Nicaea
Imperial Christianity

- Easter standardized to Sunday throughout the empire
- Calculated independently of the Jewish calendar
- Anti-Jewish rhetoric begins to appear in official language

Key Insight: Easter becomes a church-regulated calendar event, shaped by imperial concerns.

4th–6th Centuries — Expansion of Liturgical Easter
Institutional Church

- Easter season expands (Holy Week, Pentecost cycle)
- Fasting and preparation practices develop
- Pascha increasingly detached from Jewish reckoning

Key Insight: Theological truth remains, but ritual complexity increases.

Medieval Period (c. 600–1500) — Folk Customs Added
Cultural Layering

- Eggs, spring imagery, and folk practices appear
- Popular customs grow alongside church liturgy

- Easter becomes both religious and cultural

Key Insight: Symbols multiply, meanings blur.

16th Century — Reformation Responses
Divergent Approaches
- Luther: retains Easter, rejects compulsion
- Calvin: permits but warns against superstition
- Radical Reformers: often reject Easter entirely

Key Insight: Easter observance becomes a matter of conscience.

19th–21st Centuries — Modern Easter
Secularization & Revival
- Easter becomes one of the most attended church days
- Competes with consumer culture and sentimentality
- Resurrection sometimes reduced to metaphor or tradition

Key Insight: The challenge is no longer paganism, but cultural dilution.

Timeline Summary for Readers
- Passover → Commanded, covenantal, redemptive
- Resurrection → Historical, essential, apostolic
- Pascha/Easter → Developed, debated, optional as a festival

The resurrection is non-negotiable.
The festival is historical.
Discernment is required.

Footnotes

1. Oscar Cullmann, *Christ and Time* (Philadelphia: Westminster Press, 1950), 84–92.
2. James D. G. Dunn, *The Partings of the Ways* (London: SCM Press, 2006), 230–245.
3. Brant Pitre, *Jesus and the Jewish Roots of the Eucharist* (New York: Doubleday, 2011), 55–78.
4. David Instone-Brewer, *Traditions of the Rabbis from the Era of the New Testament* (Grand Rapids: Eerdmans, 2004), 112–130.
5. Paul F. Bradshaw, *Early Christian Worship* (Collegeville, MN: Liturgical Press, 2010), 87–104.
6. Andrew McGowan, *Ancient Christian Worship* (Grand Rapids: Baker Academic, 2014), 141–160.
7. Ramsay MacMullen, *Christianizing the Roman Empire* (New Haven: Yale University Press, 1984), 41–58.
8. Peter J. Leithart, *Defending Constantine* (Downers Grove, IL: IVP Academic, 2010), 215–233.
9. J. N. D. Kelly, *Early Christian Doctrines* (New York: HarperOne, 1978), 141–150.
10. N. T. Wright, *The Resurrection of the Son of God* (Minneapolis: Fortress Press, 2003), 32–84.
11. Martin Luther, *Church Postils,* Easter Sermons, in *Luther's Works,* vol. 51 (Philadelphia: Fortress Press, 1974).
12. John Calvin, I*nstitutes of the Christian Religion* 4.10.30.
13. Michael Horton, *A Better Way* (Grand Rapids: Baker Books, 2002), 89–102.

Chapter 4

SUNDAY WORSHIP: SABBATH, THE LORD'S DAY, AND THE MAKING OF A CHRISTIAN WEEK

Introduction: Why the "Day" Question Matters

Few questions in Christian practice generate as much sustained debate—across centuries, denominations, and cultures—as the question of which day Christians should regard as their primary day of worship. For some believers, Sunday worship is simply "what Christians do," inherited as an unquestioned norm. For others, Sunday is an unscriptural substitution that displaced the biblical Sabbath (the seventh day), often associated with Constantine, church councils, or anti-Judah sentiment. Still others approach the issue through the lens of Christian liberty, believing that the New Testament does not bind believers to a specific day in the way the Mosaic covenant bound Israel.

This chapter aims to treat the matter with careful balance: historically honest, biblically grounded, and pastorally responsible. It will show that Sunday worship did not appear out of nowhere in the fourth century, yet it also demonstrates that later institutional developments (especially after Constantine) significantly shaped how Sunday functioned in Christian life. The central question is not merely what Christians did, but what the New Testament requires, what church history documents, and what faithful Christ followers should avoid when navigating sacred time.

We will trace:

1. The Sabbath in the Hebrew Scriptures and Hebrew identity
2. Jesus and the Sabbath in the Gospels

3. The earliest Christian gatherings and the "first day" evidence
4. The meaning of "the Lord's Day"
5. The gradual separation between synagogue and church
6. Constantine's Sunday legislation and the imperial reshaping of worship time
7. Conciliar developments (including Laodicea) and anti-Judaic dynamics
8. Reformation and modern debates (Sabbatarian, non-Sabbatarian, and "Lord's Day" views)
9. Discernment: what faithful Christ followers should avoid

Throughout, we will keep one distinction consistently in view: the biblical Sabbath is a covenant sign for Israel, while Sunday worship developed as a Christian practice in complex historical conditions. Whether one concludes that Sunday is a new covenant obligation, a normative apostolic pattern, or a permissible tradition, the evidence must be handled carefully rather than polemically.

The Sabbath in Scripture: Creation, Covenant, and Identity

The Sabbath's roots reach deep into Israel's sacred story. In the creation narrative, God "rested" on the seventh day and sanctified it (Genesis 2:2–3). Yet Genesis does not depict Adam and Eve commanded to keep Sabbath. The explicit command appears later, in the Mosaic covenant. In Exodus 20:8–11 (the Ten Commandments), Sabbath is grounded in creation; in Deuteronomy 5:12–15, it is grounded in redemption from Egypt. The Sabbath therefore functions as both a creational pattern and a covenantal sign, integrating worship, rest, justice (including rest for servants), and identity.

Within Israel, Sabbath became a boundary marker—an embodied confession that Israel belonged to YHWH, not to Pharaoh-like economies of endless labor. Scholars note that Sabbath-keeping distinguished Jews within the ancient world and served as a powerful identity practice during exile and diaspora.[1] In Second Temple Judaic religious practices, Sabbath observance intensified as a communal marker, and disputes arose regarding what constituted legitimate Sabbath practice—disputes visible in the Gospels.

This matters because early Christians emerged from within this Judaic world. The first believers were Judahites who revered Torah, practiced synagogue rhythms, and saw Jesus as Israel's Messiah. Any Christian account of Sunday worship that ignores this Judaic matrix will inevitably misread the earliest evidence.

Jesus and the Sabbath: Fulfillment, Mercy, and Authority

The Gospels depict Jesus frequently in controversy with religious leaders concerning Sabbath observance. These controversies do not show Jesus rejecting Sabbath; rather, they show Jesus asserting messianic authority over Sabbath interpretation. He heals on the Sabbath, defends acts of mercy, and critiques legalism that burdens human life. *The Sabbath was made for man, not man for the Sabbath"* (Mark 2:27) and *"the Son of Man is lord even of the Sabbath"* (Mark 2:28) do not abolish Sabbath in the narrative world of the Gospels; they establish Jesus as the definitive interpreter and Lord of sacred time.

New Testament scholars often emphasize that Jesus' Sabbath actions signal eschatological fulfillment—the inbreaking kingdom reorients covenant signs around Himself.[2] Yet the Gospels do not explicitly state a "transfer" of Sabbath to Sunday. The shift from seventh-day Sabbath to first-day worship is not spelled out as a decree; it is discerned from patterns, theological developments, and the unfolding life of the early church.

Early Christian Practice: Evidence for First-Day Gatherings

The "First Day" Texts

Two New Testament passages are central to arguments for early

Sunday gatherings:

- Acts 20:7: "On the first day of the week… we were gathered together to break bread."
- 1 Corinthians 16:2: Paul instructs believers to set aside collections "on the first day of every week."

These texts suggest that first-day gatherings existed, at least in some communities, and that they were associated with "breaking bread" and communal life. Scholars debate how much these texts can bear. Some argue they reveal a regular Christian worship day; others see them as descriptive rather than prescriptive.[3] Still, the evidence indicates that "first day" practices arose early, and they were not dependent on Constantine.

Resurrection and the First Day

The resurrection occurred "on the first day of the week" (e.g., Matthew 28:1; Mark 16:2; Luke 24:1; John 20:1). John's Gospel also depicts appearances of the risen Christ on that day and again "eight days later" (John 20:19, 26), which some interpret as a pattern of weekly assembly. While this is not a command, it is the theological background that later Christians used to associate the first day with resurrection joy and new creation.

N. T. Wright's resurrection scholarship emphasizes that the early Christian claim was not symbolic renewal but historical victory, and that worship practices developed to proclaim this new reality.[4] Over time, the first day became a weekly rhythm in which Christians rehearsed the resurrection story, not merely annually (as with Easter).

"The Lord's Day": What Did Early Christians Mean?

Revelation 1:10 contains a pivotal phrase: "I was in the Spirit on the Lord's day." Many early Christian writers interpreted this as Sunday. But what exactly does "Lord's day" mean?

Some scholars argue that the phrase likely refers to Sunday as a recognized Christian designation by the late first century. Others caution that the term could have broader eschatological meaning ("the day of the Lord"). Yet the dominant patristic interpretation identifies it with Sunday, suggesting that Christians were already naming a day distinctively.[5]

Ignatius of Antioch (early second century) is often cited in this conversation. In one passage, he contrasts living "according to the Lord's Day" with older patterns, though interpretation is debated due to textual and translation issues.[6] Nevertheless, Ignatius provides evidence that Christians were already developing distinctive rhythms that they believed were aligned with the new covenant reality.

The Sub-Apostolic Witness: Didache, Ignatius, and Justin Martyr

When we move into the second century, evidence for Sunday worship becomes clearer.

- The Didache speaks of believers gathering and breaking bread, and some readings connect this with "the Lord's Day," though the text is not a systematic liturgical manual.[7]
- Justin Martyr (mid-second century) offers one of the most explicit early descriptions of Sunday worship in *First Apology*. He explains that Christians assemble on "the day called Sunday," reading Scripture, offering prayers, and participating in the Eucharist. Justin gives theological reasons: Sunday is connected with creation and resurrection.[8]

What should be emphasized is that Justin's witness predates Constantine by more than a century and reflects a Christian community that already viewed Sunday assembly as normal.

Liturgical historians stress that early Christian worship practices were not uniform everywhere. Some communities maintained strong Sabbath connections; others increasingly centered Sunday. Paul Bradshaw and Maxwell Johnson caution that the diversity of early practice should not be flattened into a single narrative.[9] But the overall trajectory is difficult to deny: Sunday worship became widespread well before imperial legislation.

Sabbath and Sunday in the Early Centuries: Not a Single Story

A common error in popular debates is assuming that early Christians either (a) all kept Saturday Sabbath until Constantine changed it, or (b) all abandoned Sabbath immediately after the resurrection. The historical reality is more complex.

Hebrew Christians and Sabbath Continuity

Hebrew Christians often continued to honor Sabbath, attend synagogue, and maintain Judaic rhythms, while also confessing Jesus as Messiah. The book of Acts depicts Hebrew believers participating in temple life (Acts 2–3) and attending synagogue contexts (Acts 13; 17). This continuity does not necessarily mean Christians viewed Sabbath as binding on Gentiles; it means early Christian identity existed within Judaic life.

Scholars like James D. G. Dunn and Daniel Boyarin emphasize that the "parting of the ways" between Judaism and Christianity was gradual, not instant.[10] In such a world, Christian time-practices could be hybrid: Sabbath piety plus first-day celebration, depending on community context.

Gentile Christians and Distinctive Christian Identity

As Gentile Christianity expanded, communities increasingly defined themselves apart from synagogue calendars. Social pressures, persecution, and disputes contributed to this shift. Some Christian leaders sought to distinguish Christian worship from Judaic practices, sometimes in unhealthy ways that fed anti-Judaic rhetoric.

This dynamic becomes especially visible after the Hebrew revolts (66–73, 132–135 CE) and the increasing marginalization of Jews in the empire. The church's attempt to distance itself from Judaic suspicion sometimes included distancing from Judaic sacred time.[11]

Constantine and Sunday Legislation: What Changed and What Didn't

Constantine's 321 CE Sunday Law

In 321 CE, Constantine issued a civil decree instructing urban populations to rest "on the venerable day of the sun," while allowing agricultural labor as needed.[12] This law is often invoked to argue that Constantine "changed the Sabbath to Sunday." Historically, that claim overstates what the law did.

Constantine's decree did not create Christian Sunday worship out of nothing—Sunday assemblies existed long before him. But Constantine's legislation did change the social meaning of Sunday by granting it civil preference and embedding it in imperial life. Ramsay MacMullen's work on Christianization highlights that imperial policy frequently functioned through pragmatic governance: unifying populations, stabilizing social order, and reinforcing the emperor's role as patron of religion.[13]

A Mixed Vocabulary: "Day of the Sun" and Christian Meaning

Constantine's language reflects the Roman cultural world. Calling it "the day of the sun" does not automatically mean Constantine intended pagan worship; it reflects conventional terminology. Still, Christians later interpreted Sunday's significance as "the Lord's Day," tying it to resurrection and new creation.

Peter Leithart argues that Constantine's role must be interpreted with nuance—neither demonized as a pagan conspirator nor romanticized as purely spiritual.[14] The key shift is that Sunday became not only an ecclesial practice but also a civic rhythm.

This introduces a major theme for discernment: when worship patterns become state patterns, coercion and conformity pressures increase.

The Council of Laodicea and Anti-Jewish Dynamics

By the fourth century, some councils addressed Christian behavior toward Judaic practices. The Council of Laodicea (often dated mid-to-late fourth century) is frequently cited because one canon discourages Christians from "Judaizing" by resting on the Sabbath and urges honoring the Lord's Day instead.[15]

This canon does not prove that Sunday worship began then; it proves that some Christians still honored Sabbath, and the church leadership sought to regulate identity and boundaries. It also reflects the reality that anti-Judaic sentiment had entered church life in ways that should trouble faithful readers.

Modern historians and theologians increasingly emphasize that Christian identity formation in late antiquity sometimes involved defining Christianity against Judaic practices. This legacy requires sober reckoning, especially when sacred time debates become vehicles for contempt rather than truth.[16]

Theological Interpretations: Three Major Christian Positions

At this point, the historical record can be summarized: early Christian Sunday worship is documented before Constantine; Sabbath observance continued in various ways; imperial and conciliar developments increased Sunday's dominance and sometimes carried anti-Judaic rhetoric.

How should Christians interpret these facts theologically? Broadly, three positions have emerged:

Seventh-Day Sabbatarian View

This view holds that the seventh-day Sabbath remains binding, often as a creation ordinance and moral command. Some Sabbatarians argue Sunday worship is a later corruption; others allow Sunday gatherings but maintain Saturday as the commanded Sabbath.

A major scholarly advocate of a strong Sabbatarian critique is Samuele Bacchiocchi, who argues that the shift toward Sunday was influenced by anti-Judaic sentiment and Roman culture, and that Sabbath has enduring theological significance.[17] Whether one agrees with Bacchiocchi or not, his work represents an important scholarly voice that compels careful engagement rather than caricature.

"Lord's Day" View (Sunday as Christian Sabbath)

This view argues that the "Lord's Day" is the new covenant transformation of Sabbath—Sunday becomes the Christian day of rest and worship. Historically, this position developed strongly in Reformed and Puritan traditions, emphasizing continuity of moral law.

D. A. Carson's edited volume From Sabbath to Lord's Day represents a major scholarly conversation on this topic, including arguments that Sunday worship is grounded in early Christian practice and theological development.[18]

Non-Sabbatarian / Christian Liberty View

This view holds that the New Testament does not bind believers to a specific day. Christians may gather on any day; Sunday is a historically rooted tradition but not a command. Advocates often emphasize Romans 14 and Colossians 2:16–17, arguing that sacred days should not bind conscience.

Craig Keener, for instance, underscores that early Christian practice must be interpreted through the lens of new covenant freedom and the diversity of early communities.[19] Similarly, many liturgical historians emphasize that early Christian rhythms emerged organically and regionally rather than through a single apostolic decree.

Paul, Romans 14, and Colossians 2: "Days" and Conscience

Two Pauline texts shape Christian discernment:

- Romans 14:5–6: "One person esteems one day as better than another, while another esteems all days alike… Each one should be fully convinced in his own mind."
- Colossians 2:16–17: "Let no one pass judgment on you… with regard to a festival or a new moon or a Sabbath."

Interpretations vary. Some read these as directly including weekly Sabbath; others see them aimed at Hebraic calendar observances imposed on Gentiles. Either way, Paul's central concern is clear: days must not become instruments of judgment, spiritual pride, or bondage. The gospel is not advanced by calendar warfare.

N. T. Wright, in his broader Pauline work, repeatedly stresses that for Paul, covenant identity is redefined around Messiah and Spirit, not around boundary markers like circumcision or calendrical observance.[20] That does not trivialize sacred time; it locates its meaning within Christ.

What Faithful Christ Followers Should Avoid Regarding Sunday Worship

With history and theology in view, faithful Christ followers should avoid several recurrent errors:

1. Avoid historical myths
It is historically inaccurate to claim "Constantine invented Sunday worship." Sunday gatherings are documented well before the fourth century.[21] At the same time, it is also simplistic to deny that Constantine and later councils shaped Sunday's social dominance.

2. Avoid contempt toward Jews or Judaic practice
Anti-Judaic rhetoric is incompatible with the gospel and obscures Christianity's Hebrew roots. Any argument for

Sunday that depends on denigrating Sabbath as "Jewish legalism" is spiritually dangerous and historically careless.

3. <u>Avoid making a day a test of salvation</u>
Whether one worships on Saturday, Sunday, or multiple days, salvation rests in Christ—not in calendrical correctness. Paul's warnings against judgment over days should be taken seriously.

4. <u>Avoid reducing worship to attendance</u>
Whether on Sunday or Sabbath, faithful worship is not mere gathering; it is the offering of the whole life to God. A "Sunday-only Christianity" can become a weekly ritual that hides moral compromise.

5. <u>Avoid severing worship from resurrection life</u>
If Sunday worship is practiced, it should proclaim resurrection and new creation, not mere habit. If Sabbath is practiced, it should reflect trust, mercy, justice, and freedom—not legalistic control.

Conclusion: The Gospel and the Week

Sunday worship did not arise as a late imperial invention; it emerged early as Christians celebrated the resurrection in weekly rhythm. Yet the later history of Sunday shows how quickly a spiritual practice can become entangled with cultural power, political identity, and even hostility toward Judaic practices.

The New Testament does not present sacred time as the foundation of salvation. It presents Christ as the foundation, and it calls believers to worship, holiness, love, and unity. Within that framework, Christians have historically gathered on Sunday because it testifies to resurrection and new creation. Others have honored Sabbath as a creational and covenantal gift. Still others treat days with liberty, gathering when possible and refusing to bind conscience.

What must remain constant is this: time must serve Christ, not replace Him. The moment sacred time becomes sacred pride, the church loses the very Lord of the Day it claims to honor.

The next chapter will examine Lent—its roots in fasting, penitence, catechesis, and its expansion in late antiquity and medieval Christianity, along with the question of whether it represents spiritual discipline or coercive ritual.

Comparative Table: Sabbath, Lord's Day, and Christian Liberty

Category	Seventh-Day Sabbath (Saturday)	Lord's Day (Sunday Worship)	Christian Liberty View
Biblical Origin	Explicitly commanded in the Mosaic Law (Exodus 20:8-11; Deut. 5:12-15)	Not commanded explicitly; inferred from resurrection and early practice	Rooted in Pauline teaching on freedom (Romans 14; Colossians 2:16-17)
Covenantal Context	Covenant sign between God and Israel (Exodus 31:13-17)	Interpreted as new creation celebration under the new covenant	New covenant identity centered in Christ, not days
Creation Connection	Grounded in God's rest at creation	Often linked theologically to new creation/resurrection	Creation/rest principles affirmed without calendrical obligation

Practice in Jesus' Ministry	Jesus honored Sabbath but reinterpreted it through mercy and authority	No explicit Sunday command from Jesus	Jesus relativizes days by centering Himself
Apostolic Evidence	Hebrew Messianic believers continued Sabbath observance	Evidence of first-day gatherings (Acts 20:7; 1 Corinthians 16:2	Apostolic tolerance for differing practices
Early Church (1st-2nd c.)	Continued among Hebrew Messianic believers	Increasingly common among Gentile believers	Diversity of practice without schism
Imperial Influence	Marginalized in Christian empire	Reinforced by Constantine and later councils	Often articulated in reaction to coercion
Theological Emphasis	Rest, obedience, covenant faithfulness	Resurrection, new creation, eschatological joy	Freedom, conscience, unity
Primary Risk	Legalism, boundary-marker absolutism	Traditionalism, coercion, anti-Hebrew rhetoric	Individualism, loss of communal rhythm
Salvific Status	Not salvific	Not salvific	Explicitly non-salvific
Modern Advocates	Seventh-day Sabbatarians	Reformed/historic Protestant traditions	Many evangelicals and liturgical historians

Pauline Evaluation	Not binding on Gentiles	Permissible but not compulsory	Explicitly affirmed (Rom. 14)
Core Insight	Sacred time as covenant sign	Sacred time as resurrection proclamation	Sacred time serves Christ, not vice versa

Footnotes

1. E. P. Sanders, *Judaism: Practice and Belief,* 63 BCE–66 CE (London: SCM Press, 1992), 193–220.
2. Craig A. Evans, *Jesus and the Remains of His Day* (Peabody, MA: Hendrickson, 2015), 128–152.
3. Richard Bauckham, "Sabbath and Sunday in the Post-Apostolic Church," in *From Sabbath to Lord's Day,* ed. D. A. Carson (Grand Rapids: Zondervan, 1982), 251–298.
4. N. T. Wright, *The Resurrection of the Son of God* (Minneapolis: Fortress Press, 2003), 707–740.
5. David E. Aune, *Revelation 1–5,* Word Biblical Commentary 52A (Dallas: Word Books, 1997), 84–86.
6. Ignatius of Antioch, *Letter to the Magnesians* 9, in *The Apostolic Fathers,* trans. Michael W. Holmes, 3rd ed. (Grand Rapids: Baker Academic, 2007), 205–207.
7. *The Didache,* in Holmes, *The Apostolic Fathers,* 345–357.
8. Justin Martyr, *First Apology* 67, in *The First and Second Apologies,* trans. Leslie W. Barnard (New York: Paulist Press, 1997), 75–77.
9. Paul F. Bradshaw and Maxwell E. Johnson, *The Origins of Feasts, Fasts and Seasons in Early Christianity* (Collegeville, MN: Liturgical Press, 2011), 25–52.
10. James D. G. Dunn, *The Partings of the Ways: Between Christianity and Judaism and Their Significance for the Character of Christianity,* 2nd ed. (London: SCM Press,

2006), 230–260.

11. Daniel Boyarin, *Border Lines: The Partition of Judaeo-Christianity* (Philadelphia: University of Pennsylvania Press, 2004), 175–210.

12. Clyde Pharr, ed., *The Theodosian Code and Novels and the Sirmondian Constitutions* (Princeton: Princeton University Press, 1952), 53–54.

13. Ramsay MacMullen, *Christianizing the Roman Empire* (A.D. 100–400) (New Haven: Yale University Press, 1984), 41–58.

14. Peter J. Leithart, *Defending Constantine: The Twilight of an Empire and the Dawn of Christendom* (Downers Grove, IL: IVP Academic, 2010), 215–233.

15. Charles Joseph Hefele, *A History of the Councils of the Church,* vol. 2 (Edinburgh: T&T Clark, 1876), 310–313.

16. Paula Fredriksen, *Augustine and the Jews: A Christian Defense of Jews and Judaism* (New Haven: Yale University Press, 2010), 15–34.

17. Samuele Bacchiocchi, *From Sabbath to Sunday: A Historical Investigation of the Rise of Sunday Observance in Early Christianity* (Rome: Pontifical Gregorian University Press, 1977), 1–40.

18. D. A. Carson, ed., *From Sabbath to Lord's Day: A Biblical, Historical, and Theological Investigation* (Grand Rapids: Zondervan, 1982).

19. Craig S. Keener, *The IVP Bible Background Commentary: New Testament,* 2nd ed. (Downers Grove, IL: IVP Academic, 2014), 473–475.

20. N. T. Wright, *Paul and the Faithfulness of God* (Minneapolis: Fortress Press, 2013), 804–820.

21. Andrew McGowan, *Ancient Christian Worship: Early Church Practices in Social, Historical, and Theological*

Perspective (Grand Rapids: Baker Academic, 2014), 155–176.

22. Larry W. Hurtado, *Lord Jesus Christ: Devotion to Jesus in Earliest Christianity* (Grand Rapids: Eerdmans, 2003), 264–278.

Chapter 5

LENT: FASTING, REPENTANCE, AND THE RISE OF RITUALIZED PENITENCE

Introduction: A Season Both Revered and Resisted

Among all Christian observances, Lent may be the most misunderstood and internally contested. Christmas and Easter are widely recognized—even by those outside the church—but Lent often exists in an ambiguous space. Some Christians embrace it as a meaningful season of repentance, fasting, and spiritual renewal. Others reject it as an unbiblical invention tied to medieval penitential systems or Roman Catholic ritualism. Still others participate selectively, uncertain of its origins, purpose, or legitimacy.

At the heart of the debate over Lent lies a deeper theological question: What is the proper relationship between spiritual discipline and biblical authority? The New Testament clearly affirms fasting, repentance, and self-denial. Yet it nowhere commands a forty-day season preceding Easter, nor does it prescribe ashes, penitential calendars, or mandated abstentions. Lent, therefore, provides a critical case study in how Christian practices develop—often with good intentions—and how those practices can either serve or obscure the gospel.

This chapter examines Lent by tracing:

1. Fasting and repentance in Scripture
2. Early Christian ascetic practices
3. The emergence of a pre-Easter fast
4. The formalization of Lent in late antiquity
5. Medieval penitential theology and excess
6. Reformation critiques and rejections
7. Modern reinterpretations of Lent

8. What faithful Christ followers should avoid when engaging Lenten practices

Throughout, the chapter maintains a careful distinction: fasting and repentance are biblical; Lent as a structured season is historically developed. Understanding this distinction is essential for discernment rather than reaction.

Fasting and Repentance in Scripture: Biblical Foundations

Fasting in the Hebrew Scriptures

Fasting appears throughout the Hebrew Bible as a voluntary act associated with humility, repentance, mourning, and supplication. Individuals fasted in times of national crisis (Joel 2:12–17), personal distress (Psalm 35:13), or repentance (1 Samuel 7:6). Importantly, fasting was never presented as an end in itself. The prophets repeatedly warned against fasting divorced from justice and obedience (Isaiah 58:1–7; Zechariah 7:5–10).

There is no biblical command instituting a recurring fast of forty days for Israel. Even the Day of Atonement's self-affliction (Leviticus 16:29–31) does not establish a prolonged fasting season comparable to Lent. This is a critical observation: biblical fasting is situational and responsive, not calendrically mandated.

Fasting in the Ministry of Jesus

Jesus Himself fasted for forty days in the wilderness (Matthew 4:1–11), drawing clear symbolic connections to Moses (Exodus 34:28) and Elijah (1 Kings 19:8). However, Jesus never instructed His disciples to replicate this fast annually. When questioned about fasting, He emphasized its relational and eschatological dimension: fasting would be appropriate after His departure, but it must be practiced privately and sincerely (Matthew 6:16–18; 9:14–15).

Scholars note that Jesus' teaching relativizes ritual fasting by centering it on authentic devotion rather than public performance.[1]

This framework becomes crucial when later Christian fasting practices grow more elaborate and public.

Early Christian Fasting: Simplicity Before System

New Testament Evidence

The New Testament contains references to fasting (Acts 13:2–3; 14:23; 1 Corinthians 7:5), but none indicate a universal or fixed fasting calendar. Early Christian fasting was typically communal yet voluntary, undertaken in response to discernment, prayer, or crisis.

The apostolic writings also issue warnings against ascetic practices that imply spiritual superiority or salvific merit (Colossians 2:20–23; 1 Timothy 4:1–5). Paul's concern is not fasting itself, but fasting misinterpreted as a means of righteousness.

The Didache and Early Christian Rhythms

One of the earliest post-apostolic texts, the Didache, instructs Christians to fast on Wednesdays and Fridays rather than the "Jewish" fast days of Monday and Thursday.[2] This instruction demonstrates two things:

1. Early Christians did practice regular fasting.
2. They were already differentiating Christian identity from Judaic rhythms.

Yet even here, fasting is not tied to a forty-day penitential season. Liturgical historians consistently note that Lent did not exist in this form during the first two centuries.[3]

The Emergence of a Pre-Easter Fast

Short Fasts Before Pascha

By the second and third centuries, evidence appears of short fasts preceding Easter (Pascha). These fasts varied significantly—some lasted one day, others two, others a week. Irenaeus notes this diversity approvingly, emphasizing that differences in fasting length did not disrupt ecclesial unity.[4]

This diversity indicates that early Christian fasting practices were flexible and pastoral, not rigidly institutionalized. The purpose of the pre-Easter fast was preparation for baptism and Paschal celebration, not penitential payment for sin.

Baptismal Preparation and Catechesis

As Christianity expanded, Easter became a major baptismal moment. Candidates for baptism underwent instruction, fasting, and moral examination. Over time, the church extended this preparatory period, gradually standardizing it. Liturgical historians identify this baptismal context as one of the primary drivers behind what later became Lent.[5]

Thus, Lent's earliest roots are not penitential punishment but catechesis and formation.

The Forty-Day Pattern and Late Antique Development

The Symbolism of Forty

By the fourth century, a forty-day pre-Easter period became increasingly common. The number forty carried deep biblical resonance: Israel's wilderness wandering, Moses' fast, Elijah's journey, and Jesus' temptation. Church leaders interpreted Lent as a symbolic participation in Christ's wilderness testing.

Athanasius and other fourth-century bishops encouraged extended fasting seasons, viewing them as spiritually formative rather than salvific.[6] However, the length and strictness of fasting still varied by region.

Institutionalization After Constantine

As Christianity moved from persecuted minority to imperial religion, fasting practices became more regulated. Councils and bishops issued directives regarding fasting requirements, abstentions, and discipline. What had once been voluntary increasingly became expected, and in some contexts enforced.

Andrew McGowan observes that ascetic practices often intensify when Christianity gains social power, as discipline becomes a means of regulating communal identity.[7] This transition marks a turning point: Lent shifts from spiritual preparation to institutional ritual.

Medieval Lent: Penitence, Merit, and Excess

The Rise of Penitential Theology

By the medieval period, Lent became closely linked to penitential systems involving confession, satisfaction, and merit. Fasting and abstinence were often treated as compensatory acts that contributed to forgiveness or reduced temporal punishment.

Theologians such as Thomas Aquinas defended fasting as spiritually beneficial, yet even within scholastic theology there was tension between discipline as aid to virtue and discipline as meritorious work.[8] Over time, popular piety often emphasized the latter.

Social Control and Legal Enforcement

In medieval Europe, Lenten observance was sometimes enforced through civil law, with penalties for violating fasting rules. This fusion of church discipline and state power exemplifies the danger of coercive ritual. Practices intended to foster humility became instruments of conformity.

Historians consistently identify this period as one in which Lent drifted furthest from its biblical roots, becoming entangled with legalism, superstition, and fear.[9]

Reformation Critiques: Scripture, Conscience, and Freedom

Martin Luther

Martin Luther did not reject fasting outright, but he vehemently opposed compulsory Lenten observance. For Luther, fasting was acceptable only as a free discipline, never as a command binding conscience or earning righteousness.[10]

John Calvin

Calvin was even more critical. He argued that mandatory fasts and ecclesiastical calendars lacked biblical warrant and tended to obscure Christ's finished work. In the Institutes, Calvin warns that human-devised ceremonies multiply superstition when imposed as law.[11]

Radical Reformers

Anabaptists and other radical reformers often rejected Lent entirely, viewing it as emblematic of unscriptural tradition and ecclesial control. Their rejection reflects a broader concern: when discipline becomes regulation, spiritual vitality is lost.

Modern Lent: Reinterpretation and Recovery

Twentieth-Century Renewal

In the twentieth century, some Protestant traditions reintroduced Lent—not as penitential obligation, but as intentional spiritual formation. This "recovered Lent" emphasizes prayer, generosity, Scripture reading, and simplicity.

Liturgical scholars note that this recovery often strips Lent of its medieval excess while retaining its formative intent.[12] Yet tensions remain, especially among evangelicals wary of ritualism.

Contemporary Critiques

Modern theologians such as Michael Horton warn that Lent can subtly reintroduce works-oriented spirituality if not carefully framed.[13] Others argue that Lent risks creating a two-tier spirituality, where intensity is seasonal rather than lifelong.

What Faithful Christ Followers Should Avoid Regarding Lent

From Scripture and history, several cautions emerge:

1. <u>Avoid treating Lent as biblically mandated</u>
   Scripture commands repentance and fasting, not a forty-day season.
2. <u>Avoid works-based penitence</u>
   Christ's atonement is sufficient; discipline flows from grace, not toward it.
3. <u>Avoid coercion of conscience</u>
   Voluntary discipline honors Christ; enforced ritual dishonors Him.
4. <u>Avoid seasonal holiness</u>
   Repentance and self-denial are lifelong disciplines, not annual performances.
5. <u>Avoid judging others</u>
   Romans 14 applies as much to Lent as to any other observance.

Conclusion: Discipline Without Distortion

Lent stands as a vivid example of how Christian practices can emerge from sincere spiritual aims yet drift into distortion when detached from Scripture and freedom. Fasting, repentance, and self-examination are profoundly biblical. Lent, however, is a historical structure that may serve or hinder those aims depending on how it is understood and practiced.

Faithful Christ followers are not called to reject discipline, nor to embrace ritual uncritically. They are called to walk in the freedom of the gospel, practicing disciplines that point to Christ rather than replace Him.

The next chapter will examine All Saints' Day, tracing the remembrance of martyrs, the rise of saint veneration, prayer for the dead, and the development of All Hallows' observance—once again asking where memory ends and mediation begins.

Footnotes

1. Craig S. Keener, *The Gospel of Matthew* (Grand Rapids: Eerdmans, 2009), 233–240.
2. *The Didache,* in Michael W. Holmes, *The Apostolic Fathers,* 3rd ed. (Grand Rapids: Baker Academic, 2007), 352–353.
3. Paul F. Bradshaw and Maxwell E. Johnson, *The Origins of Feasts, Fasts and Seasons in Early Christianity* (Collegeville, MN: Liturgical Press, 2011), 54–78.
4. Irenaeus, cited in Eusebius, *Ecclesiastical History* 5.24.
5. Thomas J. Talley, *The Origins of the Liturgical Year* (Collegeville, MN: Liturgical Press, 1991), 182–200.
6. Athanasius, *Festal Letters,* trans. David Brakke (Liverpool: Liverpool University Press, 2010).
7. Andrew McGowan, *Ancient Christian Worship* (Grand Rapids: Baker Academic, 2014), 176–195.
8. Thomas Aquinas, *Summa Theologiae,* II–II, Q.147.
9. Eamon Duffy, *The Stripping of the Altars* (New Haven: Yale University Press, 1992), 41–65.
10. Martin Luther, *The Freedom of a Christian,* in *Luther's Works,* vol. 31.
11. John Calvin, *Institutes of the Christian Religion* 4.12.19.
12. Gordon W. Lathrop, *Holy Things* (Minneapolis: Fortress Press, 1993), 73–91.
13. Michael Horton, *A Better Way* (Grand Rapids: Baker Books, 2002), 103–118.
14. Jaroslav Pelikan, *The Christian Tradition*, vol. 1 (Chicago: University of Chicago Press, 1971), 155–178.

15. Ramsay MacMullen, *Christianizing the Roman Empire* (New Haven: Yale University Press, 1984), 65–88.
16. N. T. Wright, *After You Believe* (New York: HarperOne, 2010), 59–76.
17. Everett Ferguson, *Early Christians Speak* (Abilene, TX: ACU Press, 1999), 71–88.
18. Alister E. McGrath, *Historical Theology* (Oxford: Blackwell, 1998), 93–112.
19. Lester Ruth, *A Little Course in Christian Worship* (Nashville: Abingdon, 2014), 64–79.
20. Scot McKnight, *Fasting* (Nashville: Thomas Nelson, 2009), 21–54.

Chapter 6

ALL SAINTS' DAY: MARTYRS, MEMORY, AND THE QUESTION OF MEDIATION

Introduction: Remembering the Faithful—or Crossing a Line?

Among Christian observances, All Saints' Day (and its closely related companion, All Souls' Day) raises some of the most sensitive theological questions. Unlike Christmas or Easter—which focus on the life and work of Christ—All Saints' Day centers on the people of God, particularly those who have died in faith. For some Christians, this observance is a beautiful act of remembrance, gratitude, and continuity with the "great cloud of witnesses" (Hebrews 12:1). For others, it represents a dangerous drift from remembrance into veneration, and from honoring the faithful into practices that appear to mediate between believers and God apart from Christ.

At stake in this discussion are several foundational Christian convictions:

- the uniqueness of Christ as the sole mediator (1 Timothy 2:5),
- the nature of the communion of saints,
- the legitimacy of prayer for or to the dead, and
- the boundaries between memory, honor, intercession, and worship.

This chapter traces the development of All Saints' Day by examining:

1. The biblical foundations for remembering the faithful
2. Martyrdom and memory in the early church
3. The emergence of saint veneration

4. The development of All Saints' and All Souls' Days
5. Prayer for the dead and medieval theology
6. Reformation critiques and divisions
7. Modern interpretations and practices
8. What faithful Christ followers should avoid

As in previous chapters, the guiding distinction remains essential: remembering the faithful is biblical; ritualized veneration and mediation are historically developed and theologically contested.

Biblical Foundations: Memory, Witness, and Honor

Remembering the Faithful in Scripture

Scripture consistently affirms the importance of remembering those who have lived faithfully before God. The Old Testament preserves the memory of patriarchs, prophets, and leaders—not to invoke them, but to learn from their faithfulness (Psalm 105; Nehemiah 9). Hebrews 11 provides the clearest New Testament example: a sustained remembrance of faithful figures whose lives testify to trust in God across generations.

Crucially, Hebrews 11–12 does not encourage prayer to these figures, nor does it present them as intermediaries. Rather, their memory functions pedagogically and motivationally: "since we are surrounded by so great a cloud of witnesses… let us run with endurance" (Hebrews 12:1). The focus remains forward-facing, grounded in Christ Himself, who is named immediately as "the founder and perfecter of our faith" (Hebrews 12:2).

The Exclusivity of Christ's Mediation

The New Testament is explicit that Christ alone mediates between God and humanity: "For there is one God, and there is one mediator between God and men, the man Christ Jesus" (1 Timothy 2:5). This affirmation forms the theological boundary that all later remembrance practices must respect.

Any Christian observance involving the dead must therefore be evaluated by a central question:

Does this practice honor the faithful as examples, or does it functionally assign them a mediating role that belongs to Christ alone?

Martyrdom and Memory in the Early Church

The Age of Martyrs

In the first three centuries, Christianity was marked by intermittent persecution. Martyrdom—bearing witness unto death—became one of the most powerful expressions of Christian faithfulness. Early Christians preserved accounts of martyrs not as objects of worship, but as testimonies of courage and hope in resurrection.

Texts such as The Martyrdom of Polycarp demonstrate how early Christians remembered martyrs: their deaths were commemorated annually, often at the site of burial, through Scripture reading, prayer, and Eucharist.[1] These commemorations focused on God's grace sustaining the martyr, not on the martyr as a source of grace.

Everett Ferguson notes that early martyr remembrance functioned primarily as corporate encouragement, reinforcing hope in resurrection rather than establishing cultic devotion.[2] At this stage, the line between memory and veneration had not yet been crossed.

Anniversary Commemorations

By the second and third centuries, churches began keeping anniversaries of martyrs' deaths (often called their dies natalis, "birth into heaven"). These were localized observances, not universal feasts. Importantly, prayers were offered to God, thanking Him for the witness of the martyr—not to the martyr themselves.

This early practice provides an important corrective to simplistic claims that all later saint observances are pagan. The roots lie in Christian suffering and hope, not in pre-Christian religious cults.

From Memory to Veneration: A Subtle Shift

The Post-Constantinian Context

After Christianity gained legal status and later imperial favor in the fourth century, martyrdom declined sharply. Without ongoing persecution, the church's relationship to martyr memory changed. Sites associated with martyrs became pilgrimage destinations, and relics (bones, clothing, objects) were increasingly treated as conduits of blessing.

Peter Brown's seminal study *The Cult of the Saints* demonstrates how this shift occurred gradually. Saints were increasingly viewed as heavenly patrons who could intercede for the living, especially in a world where earthly patronage was central to social life.[3] What began as remembrance became relational: saints were no longer merely examples but perceived advocates.

Theological Rationales

Church fathers such as Augustine attempted to articulate careful distinctions. Augustine insisted that worship *(latria)* belongs to God alone, while honor *(dulia)* may be given to saints.[4] Yet in popular practice, these distinctions were often blurred. Prayers requesting saints' intercession became common, even as official theology tried to maintain Christ's unique mediatorship.

This tension—between formal doctrine and popular devotion—defines much of the subsequent history of All Saints' observance.

The Emergence of All Saints' Day

From Local to Universal Commemoration

Originally, saints were commemorated locally on the anniversary of their deaths. Over time, the growing number of martyrs and holy figures made individual observances impractical. By the fourth century, churches began experimenting with collective commemorations of all martyrs.

In the Eastern Church, a collective feast of all saints appears by the fourth century, often celebrated after Pentecost. In the Western Church, the development followed a different trajectory. By the eighth and ninth centuries, November 1 emerged as All Saints' Day, eventually standardized under Pope Gregory IV.[5]

The intent was practical and pastoral: to honor all faithful witnesses, including those unknown or unrecorded. In principle, this was an extension of earlier martyr memory—not a theological innovation.

All Souls' Day and Prayer for the Dead

The Rise of All Souls' Day

Closely linked to All Saints' Day is All Souls' Day (November 2), which focuses explicitly on the dead who are believed to be undergoing purification. This observance developed in the medieval West and is inseparable from evolving doctrines of purgatory.

Prayer for the dead has ambiguous biblical grounding. While 2 Maccabees 12:44–45 (a deuterocanonical text) describes prayer for fallen soldiers, this text is not included in the Protestant canon. The New Testament contains no explicit command to pray for the dead, nor does it clearly describe post-mortem purification.

Medieval Theology and Purgatory

By the High Middle Ages, purgatory became a central feature of Western Christian theology. Prayer, almsgiving, and masses for the dead were believed to shorten the suffering of souls in purgatory. All Souls' Day functioned as a liturgical focal point for this belief.

Historians such as Jacques Le Goff demonstrate how purgatory developed gradually, shaped by pastoral concern, imagination, and institutional power.[6] While intended to emphasize God's mercy, the system also enabled abuse, fear-based piety, and financial exploitation.

Reformation Responses: Memory Without Mediation

Martin Luther

Martin Luther affirmed the value of remembering faithful believers but rejected prayer to saints and for the dead as lacking biblical warrant. For Luther, the greatest danger was obscuring the sufficiency of Christ's atonement and mediation.[7]

John Calvin

Calvin was more sharply critical. He argued that saint veneration had become a functional replacement for Christ, turning saints into semi-divine figures in popular devotion. Calvin insisted that honoring saints as examples was legitimate, but invoking them was idolatrous.[8]

Protestant Divergence

As a result, Protestant traditions diverged sharply from Catholic and Orthodox practice. Many eliminated All Saints' Day entirely; others retained it as a day of remembrance rather than intercession. Anglican traditions often preserved All Saints' Day in this latter sense, emphasizing gratitude and witness rather than mediation.

Modern Observances and Ecumenical Tensions

Catholic and Orthodox Practice

In Roman Catholic and Eastern Orthodox traditions, All Saints' Day remains a significant feast, though theological framing varies. Official teaching continues to insist on Christ's unique mediation, while affirming the intercessory prayers of saints as participation in the communion of the church.

Protestant and Evangelical Reconsiderations

Some Protestant communities have reclaimed All Saints' Day as a time to remember the faithful dead within their own congregations—

reading names, lighting candles, and giving thanks to God. In these contexts, the day functions pastorally without invoking saintly mediation.

Liturgical theologians argue that such practices can strengthen communal memory if carefully framed within a Christ-centered theology.[9]

What Faithful Christ Followers Should Avoid Regarding All Saints' Day

From Scripture and history, several cautions emerge:

1. Avoid assigning mediatorial roles to the dead
   Christ alone intercedes as mediator.
2. Avoid blurring honor and worship
   Gratitude must never become invocation.
3. Avoid fear-based or transactional spirituality
   Practices implying post-mortem bargaining undermine grace.
4. Avoid neglecting biblical boundaries
   Scripture governs remembrance, not sentiment or tradition.
5. Avoid judging across traditions
   Differences in remembrance should be addressed with truth and love.

Conclusion: Remembering the Faithful, Exalting Christ

All Saints' Day illustrates both the beauty and the danger of Christian memory. Remembering the faithful can strengthen hope, deepen gratitude, and connect believers to the larger story of God's work through His people. Yet when remembrance crosses into mediation, the gospel's clarity is threatened.

Faithful Christ followers are called to remember the saints—but always in such a way that Christ remains preeminent. The dead are witnesses, not mediators; examples, not advocates. When memory leads us to greater trust in Christ alone, it fulfills its purpose.

The next chapter will bring this section of the book toward synthesis, examining paganism claims, cultural adaptation, and how Christians can practice discernment without fear or reactionary rejection.

Footnotes

1. *The Martyrdom of Polycarp,* in Michael W. Holmes, *The Apostolic Fathers,* 3rd ed. (Grand Rapids: Baker Academic, 2007), 231–240.
2. Everett Ferguson, *Early Christians Speak* (Abilene, TX: ACU Press, 1999), 103–120.
3. Peter Brown, *The Cult of the Saints* (Chicago: University of Chicago Press, 1981), 1–22.
4. Augustine, *City of God* 8.27.
5. Thomas J. Talley, *The Origins of the Liturgical Year* (Collegeville, MN: Liturgical Press, 1991), 190–210.
6. Jacques Le Goff, *The Birth of Purgatory* (Chicago: University of Chicago Press, 1984), 3–28.
7. Martin Luther, *Smalcald Articles,* Part II, Article II.
8. John Calvin, *Institutes of the Christian Religion* 3.20.21–27.
9. Gordon W. Lathrop, *Holy Things* (Minneapolis: Fortress Press, 1993), 109–128.
10. Jaroslav Pelikan, *The Christian Tradition,* vol. 1 (Chicago: University of Chicago Press, 1971), 122–148.
11. Alister E. McGrath, *Historical Theology* (Oxford: Blackwell, 1998), 93–112.
12. Paula Fredriksen, *Augustine and the Jews* (New Haven: Yale University Press, 2010), 85–102.
13. N. T. Wright, *Surprised by Hope* (New York: HarperOne, 2008), 161–178.

14. Robert Wilken, *The Spirit of Early Christian Thought* (New Haven: Yale University Press, 2003), 107–125.

15. Gary Macy, *The Theologies of the Eucharist in the Early Scholastic Period* (Oxford: Oxford University Press, 1984), 34–52.

16. Eamon Duffy, *The Stripping of the Altars* (New Haven: Yale University Press, 1992), 89–110.

17. Lester Ruth, *A Little Course in Christian Worship* (Nashville: Abingdon, 2014), 83–99.

18. Craig S. Keener, *The IVP Bible Background Commentary: New Testament* (Downers Grove, IL: IVP Academic, 2014), 557–560.

19. J. N. D. Kelly, *Early Christian Doctrines* (New York: HarperOne, 1978), 486–503.

20. Mark S. Kinzer, *Postmissionary Messianic Judaism* (Grand Rapids: Brazos Press, 2005), 201–215.

PART III

PAGANISM, POLEMICS, AND PASTORAL WISDOM

Chapter 7

PAGANISM, SYNCRETISM, AND CULTURAL ADAPTATION: DISCERNMENT WITHOUT FEAR

Introduction: The Most Persistent Accusation

Few claims have shaped modern Christian suspicion of historic observances more than the charge of paganism. Christmas is said to be Saturnalia in disguise. Easter is alleged to be rooted in fertility goddesses. Sunday worship is blamed on sun worship. Lent is dismissed as ascetic superstition. All Saints' Day is equated with ancestor veneration. These claims circulate widely—especially in online spaces—and are often presented with great certainty but little historical precision.

Behind these accusations lies a deeper concern that is both understandable and legitimate: How does the church remain faithful to God while living in cultures already filled with religious meaning? Scripture repeatedly warns against idolatry, syncretism, and the adoption of pagan worship (Deuteronomy 12:29–32; 1 Corinthians 10:14–22). At the same time, Scripture also shows God working redemptively within cultures, languages, and symbols that predate Israel and the church.

This chapter addresses paganism claims directly—not to dismiss them reflexively, nor to validate them uncritically, but to clarify categories, correct historical errors, and provide a biblical framework for discernment. It argues that much contemporary fear is fueled not by evidence but by conflation: equating cultural overlap with religious continuity, and adaptation with apostasy.

The chapter will examine:

1. What paganism actually means in historical terms
2. The biblical concept of syncretism
3. Cultural adaptation in Scripture itself
4. How early Christianity engaged pagan cultures
5. Where Christian observances absorbed cultural elements
6. Where legitimate boundaries were crossed
7. How to evaluate paganism claims responsibly
8. What faithful Christ followers should avoid—without fear-driven rejection

Defining Paganism: Precision Matters

Paganism as Religion, Not Aesthetic

Historically, paganism refers to polytheistic religious systems involving the worship of gods associated with nature, fertility, war, the sun, the moon, or local territories. Pagan religion was not merely symbolic or seasonal; it involved sacrifice, ritual appeasement, divination, and covenantal allegiance to deities.

This distinction is critical. A tree, an egg, a day of the week, or a seasonal festival is not pagan by itself. It becomes pagan when it is embedded in worship offered to false gods. Scripture consistently condemns the worship of other gods—not neutral objects divorced from cultic meaning.

Modern discourse often collapses this distinction, labeling any pre-Christian symbol as inherently pagan. This approach is historically unsustainable and biblically inconsistent.

The Fallacy of Parallelomania

Historians warn against a methodological error known as parallelomania—the assumption that similarity equals dependence. The mere fact that two cultures share symbols (light, rebirth, water, meals, sacrifice) does not prove one borrowed religious meaning from the other.

Pagan Parallels: Syncretism, Adaptation, or Misinterpretation?

Human societies share agricultural rhythms, seasonal awareness, and symbolic language. Christianity's emergence into a world already saturated with meaning does not automatically imply syncretism. Transmission must be demonstrated, not assumed.

Syncretism in Scripture: A Theological Category

What the Bible Condemns

Scripture is unambiguous in its condemnation of syncretism—the blending of worship of YHWH with the worship of other gods. Israel's repeated failures involved not aesthetic borrowing but divided allegiance (Exodus 32; 1 Kings 18; Hosea 2).

In the New Testament, Paul warns against participating in pagan temple feasts because they involve communion with demons (1 Corinthians 10:20–21). The issue is not cultural proximity but cultic participation.

What the Bible Does Not Condemn

Scripture does not condemn the reuse of language, time, or material culture when those elements are reoriented toward God. The Bible itself uses imagery drawn from surrounding cultures—thrones, crowns, covenants, kingship—without adopting pagan theology.

Thus, the biblical test is not origin but allegiance.

Cultural Adaptation in Scripture Itself

Israel's Redeemed Borrowing

Many features of Israel's worship share external similarities with ancient Near Eastern practices—altars, sacrifices, priesthood, incense, sacred space. Yet Israel's worship was radically redefined by monotheism, covenant ethics, and moral holiness.

God did not invent religious forms ex nihilo; He redeemed and transformed existing forms to reveal Himself. This pattern establishes a biblical precedent for adaptation without compromise.

The New Testament and Cultural Translation

The New Testament continues this pattern. The gospel is preached in Greek, framed with philosophical language (logos, conscience), and communicated through Roman roads and civic structures. Paul explicitly adapts his rhetoric depending on audience (1 Corinthians 9:19–23).

This adaptive strategy does not dilute the gospel; it advances it.

Early Christianity and Pagan Cultures

Christians Did Not Hide Pagan Worship

One of the most overlooked historical facts is that early Christians were explicitly accused of rejecting pagan worship, often at great cost. They refused to sacrifice to Roman gods, declined participation in civic religious rites, and rejected emperor worship—actions that led to persecution.

If early Christianity were merely a baptized paganism, this hostility would be inexplicable.

Distinction Without Isolation

At the same time, Christians lived in pagan societies. They shared marketplaces, calendars, language, and social customs. Over time, they reinterpreted time and memory around Christ—resurrection, incarnation, martyrdom—without reintroducing pagan gods.

This distinction—living within culture without worshiping its gods—is crucial.

Evaluating Common Paganism Claims

Calendar Overlap

The claim that Christian feasts occur near pagan festivals proves little. Agricultural societies mark time similarly. Overlap does not demonstrate theological continuity unless evidence shows intentional adoption of pagan worship.

Pagan Parallels: Syncretism, Adaptation, or Misinterpretation?

Symbolic Similarities

Light, rebirth, meals, water, and trees appear across cultures because they reflect shared human experience, not shared religious allegiance. Christianity reassigns meaning to these symbols in light of Christ.

Linguistic Confusion

Words often outlive their original meanings. The fact that English names days after Roman gods (Sunday, Thursday) does not mean modern Christians worship those gods. Language evolves faster than theology.

Where the Church Did Cross Boundaries

A balanced approach must also acknowledge real failures.

Folk Religion and Superstition

At various points, popular Christianity absorbed practices that blurred the line between devotion and magic—relic veneration, transactional prayer, fear-based rituals. These developments deserve critique, not denial.

Power and Coercion

When observances became enforced by state or church power, spiritual practices often lost their voluntary, formative character. Coercion is incompatible with gospel freedom.

Loss of Christ-Centered Focus

Any observance—Christian or otherwise—that displaces Christ's sufficiency risks becoming functionally idolatrous, even if its origins were pure.

A Framework for Discernment

Faithful Christ followers should ask four questions of any observance:

1. Who is the object of devotion? (Christ alone, or something else?)
2. What meaning is being communicated? (Biblical truth or superstition?)
3. Is conscience being bound where Scripture does not bind it?
4. Does this practice form Christlike obedience—or replace it?

This framework avoids both reactionary rejection and uncritical acceptance.

What Faithful Christ Followers Should Avoid

1. <u>Avoid fear-based theology</u>
   Fear exaggerates threats and obscures grace.
2. <u>Avoid historical misinformation</u>
   Claims must be grounded in evidence, not repetition.
3. <u>Avoid equating culture with idolatry</u>
   Culture is the mission field, not the enemy.
4. <u>Avoid replacing discipleship with ritual</u>
   No observance substitutes for obedience.
5. <u>Avoid judging fellow believers over disputable matters</u>
   Romans 14 remains decisive.

Conclusion: Truth Without Panic

The church's history reveals neither a pure isolation from culture nor a wholesale surrender to it. It reveals a long, complex struggle to confess Christ faithfully within time, language, and memory.

Paganism is real. Syncretism is dangerous. But not every tradition is pagan, and not every adaptation is compromise. Faithful discernment requires more than slogans—it requires Scripture, historical honesty, and spiritual maturity.

The goal is not to purify Christianity of history, but to purify devotion to Christ within history.

The final chapter will bring these themes together in a comparative synthesis, offering guidance for pastors, leaders, and believers seeking to navigate Christian observance with clarity, courage, and charity.

Chapter 8

AFTER THE EVIDENCE: TRADITION, TRUTH, AND THE QUESTION OF CHRISTIAN OBSERVANCE

Introduction: When History Disturbs Certainty

For many believers, historical inquiry into Christian observances does not end with curiosity; it ends with discomfort. Learning that Christmas was not celebrated by the earliest Christians, that Easter was standardized through councils, that Sunday worship developed over time, or that Lent and All Saints' Day emerged gradually rather than apostolically can feel destabilizing. For some, these discoveries provoke anger toward the institutional church. For others, they inspire suspicion toward all tradition. Still others respond by retreating into defensive certainty, dismissing historical scholarship as irrelevant or hostile to faith.

This chapter addresses that moment of tension—the moment when historical evidence collides with inherited certainty. The goal is not to rescue tradition from scrutiny, nor to rescue skepticism from responsibility, but to guide readers through a more mature question: What does faithfulness look like after the facts are known?

Christian history does not ask to be feared, nor does it ask to be idolized. It asks to be understood. And understanding requires rejecting two false paths that repeatedly emerge whenever sacred practices are examined: uncritical acceptance and reactionary rejection. Both fail for the same reason—they replace discernment with absolutism.

Tradition and the Fear of Collapse

A recurring fear beneath objections to historical inquiry is the assumption that if a practice is shown not to be apostolic, then Christianity itself is compromised. This fear rests on a fragile view of faith—one that confuses unchanging truth with unchanging practice. Yet Scripture itself records a living, developing faith community, one that faced new questions, new contexts, and new decisions under the guidance of the Holy Spirit.

The apostolic church did not inherit a complete liturgical system from Jesus. It discerned how to live faithfully in light of Christ's resurrection, the inclusion of Gentiles, persecution, and cultural change. Acts 15 stands as a defining example: the church was forced to make a decision that Jesus never explicitly addressed—whether Gentile believers must keep the Mosaic law. The solution was neither strict traditionalism nor careless innovation, but Spirit-guided discernment rooted in Scripture and communal wisdom.

Jaroslav Pelikan reminds us that tradition is not the dead hand of the past, but the living faith of the dead—a dynamic process by which the church wrestles with truth across generations.[1] To reject all post-biblical tradition as corruption is to misunderstand how doctrine itself survived. The canon of Scripture, the doctrine of the Trinity, and the confession of Christ's two natures all emerged through historical processes. Few Christians would argue that these developments invalidate the faith.

The real question, therefore, is not whether traditions developed, but how they developed and whether they remained accountable to the gospel.

The Apostolic Measure: Continuity Without Replication

One of the most common objections raised against Christian observances is the claim that if the apostles did not practice them, then modern Christians must not either. While this objection sounds faithful, it misunderstands apostolic authority. The apostles did not function as ritual architects designing a permanent calendar. They functioned as witnesses to the risen Christ and stewards of the gospel.

The New Testament itself reflects development: church offices evolved, worship contexts shifted, and theological clarity deepened over time. As Luke Timothy Johnson notes, early Christianity was not a static system but a traditioned movement, shaped by memory, interpretation, and mission.[2] The absence of a command does not imply prohibition. Nor does development imply deviation.

This distinction is crucial. When Christian observances commemorate biblical events without claiming biblical mandate, they occupy a different category than doctrines essential to salvation. Problems arise only when historical practices are treated as divine law or when dissent is framed as disobedience rather than conscience.

Cultural Adaptation and the Myth of Pure Origins

Another objection frequently raised is that cultural adaptation equals theological compromise. This view imagines an early Christianity uncontaminated by culture, language, or symbolism—a historically impossible scenario. Christianity was born not in abstraction, but in the Judaic world of Second Temple worship and the Greco-Roman world of philosophy, rhetoric, and civic life.

The New Testament itself is written in Greek, employs Stoic and Platonic vocabulary, and assumes Roman infrastructure. Paul's sermon at the Areopagus explicitly engages pagan poets while rejecting pagan gods (Acts 17:22–31). This is not syncretism; it is contextual proclamation.

Scholars such as Andrew Walls argue that Christianity is inherently translatable—it must enter cultures in order to transform them.[3] The danger lies not in translation, but in misdirected allegiance. Syncretism occurs when worship is divided, not when symbols are reinterpreted.

This insight reframes paganism accusations. The question is not whether Christians shared a calendar, language, or season with surrounding cultures, but whether they shared worship. Historically, the early church was persecuted precisely because it refused to do so.

Where the Church Must Admit Failure

A responsible narrative must also acknowledge that the church has not always navigated tradition wisely. There were moments when spiritual disciplines became instruments of control, when observances were enforced by law, and when fear eclipsed grace. Medieval penitential systems, coercive fasting regulations, and transactional views of prayer for the dead represent genuine distortions of gospel freedom.

Eamon Duffy's work on late medieval Christianity demonstrates how popular piety often drifted from theological ideals, becoming entangled with fear, superstition, and economic exploitation.[4] These failures must not be minimized. They are part of the historical record and part of the reason modern Christians react so strongly against tradition.

Yet abuse does not negate proper use. The existence of distortion does not prove that all observance is corrupt; it proves that discernment must be ongoing.

Defending Observance Without Absolutizing It

Christian observances may be defended—not as mandates, but as historical tools the church has used to teach, remember, and form believers. They are means, not measures of faithfulness. When Christmas proclaims incarnation humility, Easter proclaims resurrection hope, Sunday worship proclaims new creation, Lent encourages repentance, and All Saints' Day remembers faithful witnesses, these practices can serve the gospel.

But when observances:

- bind conscience where Scripture does not,
- replace obedience with ritual,
- or obscure Christ's sufficiency, they must be reformed or relinquished.

This balanced defense rejects both nostalgia and nihilism. It affirms that Christianity did not lose the gospel when it developed a calendar, nor did it preserve the gospel by remaining ritually undefined. What preserved the gospel was Christ Himself, faithfully proclaimed across generations that sometimes succeeded and sometimes failed.

Conclusion: History as a Teacher, Not a Judge

History does not exist to condemn the present or to canonize the past. It exists to teach. When approached humbly, it reveals both the wisdom and the wounds of the church. Faithfulness after the facts requires neither denial nor despair, but maturity.

Christian observance must always remain secondary to Christian obedience. Tradition must serve truth, not replace it. And the church must remain free enough to reform what no longer serves Christ, while grateful enough to learn from what once did.

The next chapter will move from defense to direction—asking not how observances can be justified, but how believers should live faithfully and charitably in light of historical truth.

Footnotes

1. Jaroslav Pelikan, *The Christian Tradition: A History of the Development of Doctrine,* vol. 1 (Chicago: University of Chicago Press, 1971).
2. Luke Timothy Johnson, *The Writings of the New Testament,* 3rd ed. (Minneapolis: Fortress Press, 2010).

3. Andrew F. Walls, *The Missionary Movement in Christian History* (Maryknoll, NY: Orbis Books, 1996).
4. Eamon Duffy, *The Stripping of the Altars* (New Haven: Yale University Press, 1992).
5. Alister E. McGrath, *Historical Theology* (Oxford: Blackwell, 1998).
6. N. T. Wright, *Paul and the Faithfulness of God* (Minneapolis: Fortress Press, 2013).
7. Everett Ferguson, *Church History, Volume 1* (Grand Rapids: Zondervan, 2005).

Chapter 9

LIVING FAITHFULLY AFTER THE FACTS: DISCERNMENT, LIBERTY, AND CHRIST-CENTERED PRACTICE

Introduction: When Knowledge Demands a Way of Life

Historical knowledge creates a moral obligation. Once believers understand how Christian observances developed—how they emerged, changed, hardened, and were sometimes distorted—they can no longer appeal to ignorance. The question is no longer What happened? but How shall we now live? This chapter exists precisely at that junction, where history presses upon conscience and theology must become practice.

For many readers, the preceding chapters will have unsettled assumptions. Practices once received as unquestioned inheritances may now appear complex, contingent, and human. Others may feel vindicated in long-held suspicions about tradition. Still others may experience tension—wanting to honor Christ sincerely while unsure how to relate to practices that are neither commanded nor forbidden by Scripture. These responses are not signs of failure; they are signs of engagement. The danger lies not in wrestling with complexity, but in resolving it poorly.

This chapter argues that faithful Christian living after the facts requires three interwoven commitments: discernment shaped by Scripture, liberty guarded by love, and practices consistently re-centered on Christ Himself. Without these commitments, historical knowledge becomes either a weapon or a burden. With them, it becomes a gift that matures faith rather than destabilizing it.

Discernment as a Mark of Christian Maturity

Discernment is often misunderstood as suspicion. In reality, discernment is a form of wisdom cultivated through Scripture, prayer, and experience. The New Testament presents discernment not as optional but as essential to maturity. The author of Hebrews rebukes believers who remain dependent on simple instruction, insisting that "solid food is for the mature, for those who have their powers of discernment trained by constant practice" (Hebrews 5:14). Discernment, then, is learned, practiced, and refined over time.

Applied to Christian observances, discernment begins by recognizing categories. There is a profound difference between gospel truth and gospel tradition, between what saves and what signifies. The incarnation, crucifixion, and resurrection are saving acts of God; Christmas and Easter are historical means by which the church remembers them. Confusion arises when these categories are collapsed—when observances are treated as if they carry salvific weight, or when gospel events are dismissed because of later traditions attached to them.

N. T. Wright repeatedly emphasizes that Christian maturity involves learning to distinguish means from ends.[1] Practices exist to serve transformation; they do not produce it automatically. Discernment asks whether a practice is functioning as a servant of faith or has subtly become its substitute.

This perspective reframes the anxiety many believers feel when learning that certain observances are historically developed. The presence of development does not invalidate a practice; it simply relocates its authority. What is historically developed must remain theologically accountable.

Liberty of Conscience: The Forgotten Doctrine

Few doctrines are affirmed verbally yet violated practically as often as liberty of conscience. The apostle Paul treats conscience not as an inconvenience but as a sacred space where believers respond directly to God. Romans 14 stands as the clearest biblical treatment of this issue. Paul addresses disagreements over food and days—matters deeply tied to Jewish and Gentile identity—and refuses to resolve them by enforcing uniformity. Instead, he insists that "each one should be fully convinced in his own mind" (Romans 14:5).

Crucially, Paul does not relativize truth; he relativizes non-essential practice. He recognizes that faithful believers, equally committed to Christ, may arrive at different conclusions regarding observance. The sin he condemns is not differing practice, but judgment—the elevation of personal conviction into a universal standard.

Historically, this principle was often lost as Christianity gained institutional power. Once observances became markers of social belonging or orthodoxy, liberty of conscience gave way to coercion. John Calvin warned forcefully against this tendency, arguing that when the church binds conscience where God has not bound it, it assumes authority that belongs to God alone.[2]

Living faithfully after the facts requires recovering this doctrine in practice, not merely in theory. Some believers will observe Christmas or Lent as meaningful rhythms of devotion. Others will abstain out of conviction. Both responses can honor God—provided neither attempts to govern the conscience of the other. Where liberty is absent, fear and hypocrisy flourish. Where liberty is honored, genuine obedience becomes possible.

The Danger of Reactionary Faith

One of the most common pastoral outcomes of historical discovery is reactionary rejection. Upon learning that a practice is not biblically mandated or has been misused historically, some believers conclude that it must be abandoned entirely. While this response often arises from a sincere desire for purity, it carries its own dangers.

Reactionary faith tends to define faithfulness negatively—by what one avoids rather than by what one embodies. It can easily slide into a new legalism, where abstention becomes a badge of righteousness. Ironically, this mirrors the very problem reactionaries seek to escape: substituting external markers for inward transformation.

Alister McGrath notes that reform movements throughout Christian history often began with legitimate critique but faltered when reform hardened into rigidity.[3] The goal of reform is not to create a purer identity over against others, but to realign the church more faithfully with the gospel. When rejection becomes identity, discernment has given way to pride.

A historically informed faith must therefore resist the temptation to resolve complexity with absolutism. The presence of misuse does not require total abandonment; it requires wisdom about use.

Practices as Instruments of Formation

If Christian observances are to be retained at all, they must be understood as formative instruments, not spiritual guarantees. James K. A. Smith has argued persuasively that human beings are shaped not only by beliefs but by practices—by rhythms, habits, and repeated actions that train desire.[4] From this perspective, the church's development of structured time was not arbitrary; it was an attempt to shape Christian imagination and devotion.

Yet formative power cuts both ways. Practices can shape believers toward Christ, or they can shape them toward complacency, sentimentality, or moral compartmentalization. A Christmas that reinforces consumerism, an Easter that celebrates resurrection without repentance, a Lent that emphasizes self-denial without grace—all of these form believers poorly.

The question, therefore, is not whether practices form, but what they form. Practices must be continually evaluated by their fruit. Do they cultivate humility, love, obedience, and hope? Or do they foster nostalgia, fear, or self-satisfaction?

This evaluative posture prevents both naïve traditionalism and cynical rejection. It allows believers to say, This practice once served the church well, but no longer does so in this form, or This practice can still serve the gospel if reclaimed thoughtfully.

Teaching as an Act of Pastoral Responsibility

One of the most consistent contributors to confusion around observances is silence from leadership. When pastors and teachers assume shared understanding rather than providing instruction, they leave congregations vulnerable to misinformation, internet polemics, and reactionary teaching. Historical ignorance creates spiritual instability.

Everett Ferguson observes that much of what later became superstition flourished not because leaders intended deception, but because catechesis was neglected.[5] When believers do not know why a practice exists, they either attach false meaning to it or reject it altogether.

Living faithfully after the facts therefore requires intentional teaching—teaching that is honest about history, clear about Scripture, and patient with diversity of conscience. Such teaching does not dictate outcomes; it equips believers to make informed, faithful decisions.

This pedagogical responsibility is especially urgent in pluralistic contexts, where believers encounter competing narratives about Christianity's past. Silence cedes authority to the loudest voices, not the wisest ones.

Christ as the Interpretive Center

Throughout this book, one conviction has quietly governed every chapter: Christ Himself must remain the interpretive center of all practice. Observances exist to point to Him; when they obscure Him, they fail their purpose.

This Christ-centered criterion provides a practical test. Does a practice clarify the character and work of Christ? Does it deepen reliance on His grace? Does it foster obedience shaped by love? If so, it may be received with gratitude. If not, it must be reformed or relinquished—regardless of how ancient, beloved, or culturally entrenched it may be.

Dietrich Bonhoeffer warned against forms of religion that preserve Christian language while evacuating Christian substance.[6] A Christ-centered life resists this temptation by measuring every practice not by tradition alone, but by conformity to Christ.

This principle also guards against fear-driven spirituality. When Christ is central, believers need not panic over symbols, seasons, or calendars. Fear thrives where confidence in Christ's sufficiency falters.

Unity Without Uniformity Revisited

One of the most striking features of early Christianity, often overlooked in modern debates, is its capacity for unity amid diversity. The early church navigated differences in food laws, sacred days, and worship contexts without demanding uniform practice. Conflict arose not from diversity itself, but from attempts to enforce conformity.

Modern Christianity often reverses this pattern. Uniformity is pursued as a substitute for unity, while genuine fellowship fractures over secondary matters. Historical awareness should correct this tendency, reminding believers that the church has always lived with difference.

Unity is not achieved by erasing conviction, but by refusing to weaponize it. Paul's vision in Romans 14 is not of doctrinal relativism, but of Christ-centered charity—where believers submit their convictions to love and refuse to despise those who differ.

Faithfulness as a Way of Life

Ultimately, this book has argued that faithfulness is not measured by calendar accuracy or ritual precision, but by obedient trust in

Christ. Sacred time is meaningful only insofar as it serves sacred living. The danger facing modern Christians is not that they will observe the wrong day, but that they will substitute observance for discipleship.

Jesus did not say, "By this all people will know that you are my disciples, if you keep the right festivals." He said, "If you have love for one another" (John 13:35). Observances may support such love, but they can never replace it.

Living faithfully after the facts means embracing history without being enslaved to it, honoring tradition without absolutizing it, and practicing liberty without abandoning responsibility. It means walking forward neither as naïve traditionalists nor as cynical skeptics, but as mature disciples shaped by truth and grace.

Conclusion: The Simplicity Beyond Complexity

After all the history, all the debates, all the scrutiny of origins and developments, Christian faith returns to a disarmingly simple confession: Jesus Christ is Lord. That confession relativizes every calendar, every season, every practice.

Observances may come and go. Cultures change. Traditions evolve. Christ remains.

The task of the church is not to defend every inherited practice nor to dismantle them all, but to ensure that nothing competes with Christ for allegiance. When history is allowed to teach rather than terrify, it becomes a servant of faith rather than its enemy.

To live faithfully after the facts is not to live cautiously, but confidently—to walk in freedom, guided by Scripture, informed by history, and anchored in Christ, who is the same yesterday, today, and forever.

Footnotes

1. N. T. Wright, *Paul and the Faithfulness of God* (Minneapolis: Fortress Press, 2013).
2. John Calvin, *Institutes of the Christian Religion*, trans. Ford Lewis Battles (Louisville: Westminster John Knox Press, 1960).
3. Alister E. McGrath, *Historical Theology* (Oxford: Blackwell, 1998).
4. James K. A. Smith, *Desiring the Kingdom* (Grand Rapids: Baker Academic, 2009).
5. Everett Ferguson, *Church History, Volume 1: From Christ to Pre-Reformation* (Grand Rapids: Zondervan, 2005).
6. Dietrich Bonhoeffer, *The Cost of Discipleship* (New York: Touchstone, 1995).
7. Luke Timothy Johnson, *The Writings of the New Testament,* 3rd ed. (Minneapolis: Fortress Press, 2010).
8. Jaroslav Pelikan, *The Christian Tradition,* vol. 1 (Chicago: University of Chicago Press, 1971).

HOLDING FAST TO CHRIST IN SACRED TIME

Christian history is not a straight line of pristine purity nor a story of wholesale corruption. It is the story of a people redeemed by God, living out their faith within time, culture, memory, and human limitation. This book has traced the origins and development of major Christian observances—Christmas, Easter, Sunday worship, Lent, and All Saints' Day—not to dismantle Christianity, but to clarify it. The goal has never been suspicion for its own sake, nor defense of tradition at all costs, but discernment anchored in truth.

The Central Distinction: Event vs. Observance

One conclusion stands above all others: the saving events of the gospel are divinely revealed; the observances that commemorate them are historically developed.

- The incarnation, crucifixion, and resurrection of Jesus Christ are non-negotiable realities of the Christian faith.
- The dates, seasons, and rituals associated with remembering those realities emerged gradually as the church sought to teach, remember, and proclaim Christ in changing contexts.

Confusion enters when this distinction is lost. When observances are treated as if they were commanded events, tradition becomes law. When events are dismissed because of later traditions, history becomes a stumbling block. Faithfulness requires holding these categories together without collapsing one into the other.

Paganism Reconsidered: Fear vs. Fidelity

This study has shown that many popular claims about "pagan origins" rest on oversimplification rather than evidence. Paganism, biblically and historically defined, involves worship, sacrifice, and allegiance to other gods. Shared symbols, seasonal overlap, or linguistic coincidence do not in themselves constitute pagan worship.

At the same time, the church's history does include moments where cultural accommodation crossed into superstition, coercion, or distortion. A faithful reading of history requires rejecting both extremes:

- the claim that Christianity was secretly absorbed by paganism, and
- the claim that Christian tradition is above critique.

The New Testament never calls believers to fear culture, but it consistently calls them to test everything (1 Thessalonians 5:21). Discernment, not panic, is the biblical response.

Sacred Time and the Gospel of Grace

One of the most important theological insights emerging from this study is the New Testament's refusal to make sacred time salvific. Neither Sabbath nor Sunday, neither feast nor fast, neither season nor calendar is presented as a means of justification.

The apostle Paul's warnings remain decisive:

- Do not allow days to become instruments of judgment (Romans 14:5–6).
- Do not submit to regulations that promise spirituality but lack gospel power (Colossians 2:16–23).
- Do not return to bondage after being called into freedom (Galatians 4:9–11).

When observances serve grace, they can be helpful. When they replace grace, they become harmful—even if their intentions were once noble.

Memory, Formation, and the Risk of Ritual

Why, then, did these observances develop at all? The answer is not deception, but formation. Human beings remember through rhythm, story, and symbol. The church sought to shape Christian imagination, teach doctrine, and form disciples through structured time.

The danger is not memory itself, but ritual without discipleship. A church can celebrate Christmas without embracing incarnation humility. It can proclaim Easter while ignoring resurrection ethics. It can observe Lent without practicing repentance. It can remember saints while forgetting Christ's sole mediation.

The test of any observance is not whether it is ancient, popular, or emotionally powerful, but whether it forms believers into the likeness of Christ.

Unity Without Uniformity

Another consistent theme has been the presence of diversity within early Christianity—diversity of calendars, fasting practices, worship days, and commemorations. The earliest church often maintained unity without enforcing uniformity. Conflict arose not because diversity existed, but because power attempted to eliminate it.

This historical reality should temper modern dogmatism. Faithful Christ followers may:

- observe certain days with gratitude,
- reinterpret them with renewed biblical focus, or
- abstain from them altogether—without questioning one another's salvation or sincerity.

Unity in Christ does not require identical practices; it requires shared allegiance to the same Lord.

What Faithful Christ Followers Must Keep Central

If this book leaves the reader with one enduring conviction, let it be this:

Christ is not honored by flawless calendars, but by faithful lives.

Sacred time is meant to serve sacred devotion—not replace it. The church's calling is not to recover an imagined pristine past, nor to preserve tradition unexamined, but to walk forward with historical honesty, biblical clarity, and spiritual maturity.

Faithful Christ followers must therefore:

- keep Christ as the sole mediator,
- guard the sufficiency of His finished work,
- refuse fear-driven theology,
- practice liberty shaped by love, and
- engage history without surrendering conscience.

The Final Question

Every observance, every tradition, every practice ultimately answers one question:

Does this help me know Christ more clearly and follow Him more faithfully?

If the answer is yes, it may be received with gratitude.

If the answer is no, it must be set aside—no matter how ancient or beloved.

The goal of Christian life is not correct observance, but faithful obedience born of grace. Sacred time finds its meaning only when it bows to the Lord of time.

"So whether you eat or drink, or whatever you do, do all to the glory of God." (1 Corinthians 10:31)

That is the true measure of every day.

BIBLIOGRAPHY

Primary Sources (Ancient & Patristic)

Augustine. *The City of God.* Translated by Henry Bettenson. London: Penguin Classics, 2003.

Bede. *The Reckoning of Time.* Translated by Faith Wallis. Liverpool: Liverpool University Press, 1999.

Eusebius of Caesarea. *Ecclesiastical History.* Translated by Kirsopp Lake. 2 vols. Cambridge, MA: Harvard University Press, 1926.

Eusebius of Caesarea. *Life of Constantine.* Translated by Averil Cameron and Stuart G. Hall. Oxford: Oxford University Press, 1999.

Irenaeus. *Against Heresies.* In *The Ante-Nicene Fathers,* vol. 1. Edited by Alexander Roberts and James Donaldson. Peabody, MA: Hendrickson, 1994.

Polycarp of Smyrna. *The Martyrdom of Polycarp.* In Michael W. Holmes, *The Apostolic Fathers.* 3rd ed. Grand Rapids: Baker Academic, 2007.

Biblical Studies & New Testament Scholarship

Bradshaw, Paul F., and Maxwell E. Johnson. *The Origins of Feasts, Fasts and Seasons in Early Christianity.* Collegeville, MN: Liturgical Press, 2011.

Cullmann, Oscar. *Christ and Time: The Primitive Christian Conception of Time and History.* Philadelphia: Westminster Press, 1950.

Dunn, James D. G. *The Partings of the Ways: Between Christianity and Judaism and Their Significance for the Character of Christianity.* 2nd ed. London: SCM Press, 2006.

Instone-Brewer, David. *Traditions of the Rabbis from the Era of the New Testament.* Grand Rapids: Eerdmans, 2004.

Johnson, Luke Timothy. *The Writings of the New Testament: An Interpretation.* 3rd ed. Minneapolis: Fortress Press, 2010.

Keener, Craig S. *The IVP Bible Background Commentary: New Testament.* 2nd ed. Downers Grove, IL: IVP Academic, 2014.

Pitre, Brant. *Jesus and the Jewish Roots of the Eucharist.* New York: Doubleday, 2011.

Wright, N. T. *The Resurrection of the Son of God.* Minneapolis: Fortress Press, 2003.

Wright, N. T. *Surprised by Hope.* New York: HarperOne, 2008.

Wright, N. T. *Paul and the Faithfulness of God.* Minneapolis: Fortress Press, 2013.

Historical Theology & Doctrine

Calvin, John. *Institutes of the Christian Religion.* Translated by Ford Lewis Battles. Louisville: Westminster John Knox Press, 1960.

Kelly, J. N. D. *Early Christian Doctrines.* 5th ed. New York: HarperOne, 1978.

McGrath, Alister E. *Historical Theology: An Introduction to the History of Christian Thought.* Oxford: Blackwell, 1998.

Pelikan, Jaroslav. *The Christian Tradition: A History of the Development of Doctrine.* Vol. 1. Chicago: University of Chicago Press, 1971.

Early Church, Worship, and Liturgy

Bradshaw, Paul F. *Early Christian Worship.* Collegeville, MN: Liturgical Press, 2010.

Ferguson, Everett. *Early Christians Speak*. Abilene, TX: ACU Press, 1999.

Ferguson, Everett. *Church History, Volume 1: From Christ to Pre-Reformation*. Grand Rapids: Zondervan, 2005.

McGowan, Andrew. *Ancient Christian Worship*. Grand Rapids: Baker Academic, 2014.

Talley, Thomas J. *The Origins of the Liturgical Year*. Collegeville, MN: Liturgical Press, 1991.

Empire, Politics, and Sacred Time

Brown, Peter. *The Cult of the Saints: Its Rise and Function in Latin Christianity*. Chicago: University of Chicago Press, 1981.

Leithart, Peter J. *Defending Constantine: The Twilight of an Empire and the Dawn of Christendom*. Downers Grove, IL: IVP Academic, 2010.

MacMullen, Ramsay. *Christianizing the Roman Empire* (A.D. 100–400). New Haven: Yale University Press, 1984.

Wilken, Robert Louis. *The Spirit of Early Christian Thought*. New Haven: Yale University Press, 2003.

Medieval Christianity & Reformation Studies

Duffy, Eamon. *The Stripping of the Altars: Traditional Religion in England, 1400–1580*. New Haven: Yale University Press, 1992.

Le Goff, Jacques. *The Birth of Purgatory*. Chicago: University of Chicago Press, 1984.

Luther, Martin. *Luther's Works*. Vol. 51, *Sermons II*. Philadelphia: Fortress Press, 1974.

Paganism, Myth, and Cultural Critique

Hutton, Ronald. *Stations of the Sun: A History of the Ritual Year in Britain.* Oxford: Oxford University Press, 1996.

Walls, Andrew F. *The Missionary Movement in Christian History.* Maryknoll, NY: Orbis Books, 1996.

Modern Theology, Formation, and Practice

Bonhoeffer, Dietrich. *The Cost of Discipleship.* New York: Touchstone, 1995.

Horton, Michael. *A Better Way: Rediscovering the Drama of God-Centered Worship.* Grand Rapids: Baker Books, 2002.

Kinzer, Mark S. *Postmissionary Messianic Judaism.* Grand Rapids: Brazos Press, 2005.

Lathrop, Gordon W. *Holy Things: A Liturgical Theology.* Minneapolis: Fortress Press, 1993.

Ruth, Lester. *A Little Course in Christian Worship.* Nashville: Abingdon Press, 2014.

Smith, James K. A. *Desiring the Kingdom: Worship, Worldview, and Cultural Formation.* Grand Rapids: Baker Academic, 2009.

GLOSSARY OF TERMS

Adiaphora
A theological term meaning "things indifferent." In Christian theology, adiaphora refers to practices that are neither commanded nor forbidden by Scripture and therefore fall within the realm of Christian liberty (cf. Romans 14). Observances such as specific feast days are often treated as adiaphora.

All Saints' Day
A Christian observance commemorating all faithful believers who have died in Christ. Historically developed from early martyr remembrance, it is observed in various forms across Christian traditions. Theologically distinct from worship, it is intended for remembrance, gratitude, and encouragement rather than mediation.

All Souls' Day
A medieval Christian observance, primarily in Western Christianity, associated with prayer for the dead. Closely tied to doctrines of purgatory, it lacks explicit New Testament mandate and has been rejected or reinterpreted in many Protestant traditions.

Apostolic Authority
The teaching authority derived from the apostles of Jesus Christ, preserved in the New Testament. Apostolic authority is foundational for Christian doctrine but does not require that all later practices be exact replications of first-century forms.

Calendar Authority
The claimed right to regulate sacred time (feasts, fasts, holy days). Historically exercised by church councils and ecclesial leadership,

calendar authority must be distinguished from biblical command to avoid binding conscience improperly.

Catechesis
Instruction in the essentials of Christian faith and practice. In early Christianity, catechesis often involved preparation for baptism and included teaching on doctrine, ethics, prayer, and worship.

Christological Fulfillment
The theological conviction that Jesus Christ fulfills the Law, Prophets, and sacred history of Israel. Christian observances such as Easter (Pascha) are often understood as Christological reinterpretations rather than replacements of Jewish feasts.

Communion of Saints
A doctrine affirming the spiritual unity of all believers—living and dead—in Christ. Interpretations differ regarding whether this communion includes intercessory roles for the departed; Scripture emphasizes unity without assigning mediation to the dead.

Conscience
The internal moral awareness by which believers discern obedience to God. Scripture treats conscience as sacred and warns against violating or binding it where God has not spoken clearly (Romans 14; 1 Corinthians 8).

Constantinian Shift
The historical transition following Emperor Constantine's legalization of Christianity (4th century), marked by imperial involvement in church affairs. This period significantly shaped worship practices, calendar uniformity, and ecclesial power.

Council of Nicaea (325 CE)
An ecumenical council best known for addressing Christological doctrine but also influential in standardizing the date of Easter. Its decisions reflect theological, political, and cultural considerations of the imperial church.

Cultural Adaptation
The process by which Christian faith is expressed using the language, symbols, and structures of a particular culture without adopting its religious allegiance. Distinct from syncretism.

Dies Natalis
Latin for "birthday." In early Christian usage, it referred to the day of a martyr's death—understood as their birth into eternal life—and became the basis for early commemorations.

Discernment
The Spirit-guided ability to distinguish truth from error, essentials from non-essentials, and devotion from distraction. Discernment is a mark of spiritual maturity rather than suspicion.

Dulia / Latria
Theological terms used in Catholic theology to distinguish honor given to saints *(dulia)* from worship given to God alone *(latria)*. While doctrinally distinct, this distinction has often blurred in popular practice.

Easter (Pascha)
The Christian celebration of the resurrection of Jesus Christ. While the resurrection is central to the gospel, Easter as a fixed annual festival developed historically from Passover-linked remembrance and was later standardized.

Eschatology
The theological study of last things, including resurrection, judgment, and the consummation of God's kingdom. Early Christian eschatology emphasized living in light of Christ's resurrection and imminent return.

Festival Theology
The study of how religious festivals function theologically—whether as teaching tools, memorials, or sacramental acts. In Christianity, festivals are historically shaped rather than divinely mandated.

Formation
The process by which beliefs, habits, and desires are shaped over time. Christian formation includes doctrine, worship, discipline, and communal practices that mold believers into Christlikeness.

Incarnation
The Christian doctrine that the eternal Son of God became flesh in Jesus Christ (John 1:14). Celebrated liturgically at Christmas, the incarnation is foundational to Christian theology regardless of calendar observance.

Liturgical Year
The structured cycle of seasons and observances developed by the church to tell the story of Christ through time. Not commanded in Scripture, it emerged as a pedagogical and devotional tool.

Lent
A preparatory season of fasting, repentance, and reflection preceding Easter. Lent developed gradually in the early church and is understood as a voluntary discipline rather than a biblical requirement.

Mediator
One who stands between God and humanity. Scripture affirms Jesus Christ alone as mediator (1 Timothy 2:5), a key boundary in evaluating practices involving saints or the dead.

Observance
A religious practice or commemoration intended to remember or proclaim theological truth. Observances differ from doctrines in that they are historically developed and not inherently salvific.

Parallelomania
A methodological error in historical study that assumes similarity between practices implies direct borrowing or origin. Widely critiqued in academic scholarship.

Pascha
The Greek and Latin term for Easter, derived from the Hebrew *Pesach* (Passover). Most non-English Christian traditions retain this term, highlighting Easter's biblical roots.

Paganism
Historically, polytheistic religious systems involving worship of multiple gods through ritual, sacrifice, and allegiance. Paganism must be distinguished from shared cultural symbols or seasonal awareness.

Purgatory
A doctrinal development in medieval Western Christianity describing post-mortem purification. Not explicitly taught in the New Testament and rejected by most Protestant traditions.

Quartodeciman Controversy
An early Christian dispute over whether to commemorate Christ's

death and resurrection on Nisan 14 (Passover date) or on the following Sunday. Demonstrates early diversity in practice.

Sacred Time
Time set apart for religious remembrance or devotion. Scripture affirms God's lordship over time but does not mandate a Christian calendar beyond moral obedience.

Sabbath
The seventh day of rest commanded in the Mosaic Law. Interpreted differently across Christian traditions, with debates centering on continuity, fulfillment, and covenantal identity.

Saint
A believer set apart by God. In the New Testament, all believers are called saints; later usage narrowed the term to exemplary figures of faith.

Syncretism
The blending of worship or allegiance to multiple religious systems. Scripture consistently condemns syncretism as divided loyalty to God.

Sunday Worship / Lord's Day
The practice of Christian gathering on the first day of the week, associated with Christ's resurrection. Developed early and later reinforced through ecclesial and imperial structures.

Tradition
The transmission of belief and practice across generations. In Christian theology, tradition must remain accountable to Scripture and the gospel.

Unity Without Uniformity
A theological principle recognizing that believers may differ on non-essential practices while remaining united in Christ.

Veneration
Honor or respect given to saints or holy persons. Distinct from worship but often contested due to its potential to obscure Christ's unique role.

Works-Righteousness
The belief that salvation is earned through human effort or ritual. The New Testament consistently rejects this in favor of salvation by grace through faith.

Sacred or Syncretized?

KEY COUNCILS AND DECISIONS: HOW DOCTRINE AND SACRED TIME TOOK SHAPE

This appendix provides a concise, historically grounded overview of major church councils and ecclesial decisions that shaped Christian doctrine, worship, and sacred time. Its purpose is not to elevate councils to the level of Scripture, but to explain how the church wrestled with truth, unity, and practice in concrete historical moments.

Councils mattered because they addressed real crises—doctrinal confusion, pastoral division, political pressure, and questions Scripture did not answer explicitly. They did not create the gospel; they sought to protect and articulate it. Yet their decisions also reveal the limits of human authority and the ongoing need for discernment.

1. The Jerusalem Council (c. 49 CE)

(Acts 15)

<u>Primary Issue</u>: Must Gentile believers keep the Mosaic Law (circumcision, dietary laws) to be saved?

<u>Decision</u>: No. Salvation is by grace through faith in Jesus Christ alone. Gentile believers were not required to become Jews, though they were encouraged to avoid practices that would fracture fellowship.

<u>Significance</u>:

- Established salvation by grace as non-negotiable
- Demonstrated Spirit-led discernment where Jesus gave no explicit command
- Set a precedent for unity without uniformity

<u>Why It Matters for This Book</u>: This council provides the biblical

model for handling disputes over practice, culture, and conscience—directly informing later debates over sacred days and observances.

2. The Council of Nicaea (325 CE)

Council of Nicaea

Primary Issues:
1. The divinity of Christ (Arian controversy)
2. The date of Easter

Decisions:
- Affirmed the full deity of Christ (Nicene Creed)
- Standardized Easter observance on Sunday, calculated independently of the Jewish calendar

Significance:
- Preserved orthodox Christology
- Marked a decisive move toward calendar uniformity
- Reflected both theological concern and imperial influence

Cautions:
- Anti-Jewish rhetoric appeared in post-conciliar correspondence
- Easter was detached from direct Passover reckoning

Why It Matters: Nicaea shows how doctrinal clarity and political power can intersect—sometimes helpfully, sometimes problematically.

3. The Council of Constantinople (381 CE)

Council of Constantinople

Primary Issue: Clarifying Trinitarian doctrine, particularly the divinity of the Holy Spirit.

Decision: Expanded and reaffirmed the Nicene Creed, solidifying orthodox Trinitarian theology.

Significance:
- Completed the classical formulation of the Trinity
- Reinforced doctrinal unity across the empire

<u>Why It Matters:</u> This council reminds readers that doctrinal development was necessary to guard biblical truth—not to replace it.

4. The Council of Ephesus (431 CE)

Council of Ephesus
<u>Primary Issue</u>: The person of Christ—specifically whether Mary could be called Theotokos ("God-bearer").
<u>Decision</u>: Affirmed the unity of Christ's divine and human natures in one person.
<u>Significance</u>:
- Protected Christological orthodoxy
- Elevated Marian language (with later devotional consequences)

<u>Why It Matters:</u> Shows how Christ-centered decisions can later influence broader devotional practices, sometimes beyond their original intent.

5. The Council of Chalcedon (451 CE)

Council of Chalcedon
<u>Primary Issue</u>: How Christ's divine and human natures relate.
<u>Decision</u>: Defined Christ as fully God and fully man, "without confusion, change, division, or separation."
<u>Significance</u>:
- Became a cornerstone of orthodox Christology
- Also contributed to enduring divisions with some Eastern churches

<u>Why It Matters:</u> Illustrates both the necessity and cost of doctrinal precision.

6. Regional Councils and the Development of the Christian Calendar
Council of Laodicea (c. 363–364 CE)

Council of Laodicea
Key Decisions:
- Discouraged Sabbath observance in favor of Sunday worship
- Reflected growing separation from Judaic practices

Significance:
- Formalized Sunday preference
- Reinforced theological and social distancing from Judaic practices

Why It Matters: Helps explain how Sunday worship became normative, not by biblical command but ecclesial decision.

7. The Rise of Lent and Penitential Systems (4th–7th Centuries)

Not a Single Council, but a Process
Key Developments:
- Pre-baptismal fasting expanded into a universal season
- Length and rigor of Lent standardized gradually
- Penitential systems emerged alongside it

Significance:
- Lent became a tool for formation and discipline
- Also risked works-based spirituality

Why It Matters: Demonstrates how voluntary practices can harden into expectations.

8. Medieval Councils and the Doctrine of Purgatory

Second Council of Lyons (1274)
Council of Florence (1439)
Primary Issue: Clarification of purgatory and prayer for the dead.
Decisions:
- Affirmed purgatory as doctrine in Western Christianity
- Reinforced practices associated with All Souls' Day

<u>Why It Matters:</u> These decisions shaped medieval piety and provoked later Reformation critique.

9. The Council of Trent (1545–1563)

Council of Trent
<u>Primary Issues:</u>
- Protestant Reformation challenges
- Authority of Scripture and tradition
- Justification, sacraments, saints, and observances

<u>Decisions:</u>
- Reaffirmed Catholic doctrine on tradition, saints, purgatory, and liturgical calendar
- Rejected Protestant reforms

<u>Significance:</u>
- Solidified confessional divisions
- Clarified Roman Catholic positions still held today

<u>Why It Matters:</u> Trent represents the moment when diversity hardened into denominational separation.

10. Reformation Confessions (16th Century)

Though not councils in the same sense, Protestant confessions functioned similarly.
- Augsburg Confession (1530) – Allowed festivals as long as conscience was not bound
- Westminster Confession (1646) – Rejected holy days not instituted by Scripture

<u>Why It Matters:</u> These documents shaped Protestant skepticism toward sacred calendars while preserving liberty of conscience.

11. Key Patterns Across the Councils

Across centuries, several patterns emerge:

1. Doctrine precedes devotion
   Councils addressed Christology before calendars.
2. Unity often motivated decisions
   Sometimes at the expense of diversity.
3. Political power influenced outcomes
   Especially after Constantine.
4. Practices hardened over time
   What began as pastoral tools sometimes became requirements.
5. Scripture remained central—but interpreted through context

Concluding Reflection

Church councils were not villains nor infallible heroes. They were gatherings of sincere, limited, and often courageous believers seeking to guard the truth of the gospel in turbulent times. Their decisions shaped Christianity profoundly—for good and, at times, with unintended consequences.

Understanding these councils equips modern believers to:

- respect history without idolizing it
- value unity without enforcing uniformity
- honor doctrine without binding conscience

Above all, it reminds us that Christ—not councils—is Lord of the church.

Appendix C

DISCUSSION QUESTIONS BY CHAPTER

Chapter 1 – Christmas: Incarnation, History, and Sacred Memory

1. Why is the incarnation central to Christian theology regardless of when (or whether) Christmas is observed?
2. What assumptions did you previously hold about the origins of Christmas, and how did this chapter challenge or confirm them?
3. How does distinguishing between a biblical event and a historical observance help clarify debates about Christmas?
4. In what ways can Christmas observance enrich faith—and in what ways can it distract from Christ?
5. How should Christians respond when historical facts unsettle long-held traditions?

Chapter 2 – Christmas Expanded: Santa Claus, Folklore, and Cultural Layering

1. How did figures like Saint Nicholas evolve into modern Santa Claus, and why is that distinction important?
2. What dangers arise when folklore overshadows theology in Christian observance?
3. Is it possible for cultural symbols to coexist with Christian meaning without replacing it? Why or why not?
4. How should Christian parents and leaders navigate cultural Christmas traditions responsibly?
5. Where should faithful Christ followers draw boundaries between celebration and commercialization?

Chapter 3 – Easter: Resurrection, Passover, and the Struggle for Sacred Time

1. Why is the resurrection essential to Christian faith even without an annual festival?
2. How does understanding Easter's connection to Passover reshape its theological meaning?
3. What does the Quartodeciman controversy reveal about early Christian diversity?
4. How did imperial power influence Easter observance, and what lessons does that hold for today?
5. What aspects of modern Easter observance risk obscuring resurrection power?

Chapter 4 – Sunday Worship: Sabbath, Resurrection, and the Lord's Day

1. How does the New Testament portray early Christian gathering practices?
2. What is the difference between biblical command and apostolic pattern regarding worship days?
3. How did Constantine's legislation affect Sunday observance—and how is that often misunderstood?
4. Can Christians faithfully worship on different days without compromising unity?
5. How should Romans 14 guide conversations about Sabbath and Sunday today?

Chapter 5 – Lent: Repentance, Discipline, and the Risk of Legalism

1. What biblical foundations exist for fasting and repentance, even without a mandated season?
2. How did Lent develop historically, and why does that matter?

3. When does spiritual discipline become legalism?
4. Can voluntary disciplines deepen faith without becoming works-based righteousness?
5. How might Lent be practiced (or declined) in a way that honors Christian liberty?

Chapter 6 – All Saints' Day: Memory, Martyrs, and Mediation

1. What is the biblical basis for remembering faithful believers who have gone before us?
2. How did early martyr remembrance differ from later saint veneration?
3. Why is Christ's sole mediatorship such a crucial theological boundary?
4. How do different Christian traditions interpret the "communion of saints"?
5. How can remembrance strengthen faith without drifting into unbiblical mediation?

Chapter 7 – Paganism, Syncretism, and Cultural Adaptation

1. How does this chapter redefine paganism in a more historically precise way?
2. What is the difference between cultural adaptation and syncretism?
3. Why are pagan-origin claims often persuasive even when historically weak?
4. How does Scripture model engagement with culture without compromise?
5. How can fear distort discernment in conversations about tradition?

Chapter 8 – After the Evidence: Tradition, Truth, and Christian Observance

1. Why do historical discoveries about Christian practices feel threatening to some believers?
2. How does this chapter help balance respect for tradition with accountability to Scripture?
3. What dangers exist in reactionary rejection of all tradition?
4. How can observances be defended without being absolutized?
5. In what ways should history function as a teacher rather than a judge of faith?

Chapter 9 – Living Faithfully After the Facts: Discernment and Liberty

1. What responsibilities come with greater historical and theological knowledge?
2. How does liberty of conscience protect unity in the church?
3. Why is discernment a mark of maturity rather than suspicion?
4. How can practices shape believers—for better or worse?
5. What does it mean practically to keep Christ at the center of all observance?

Final Conclusion – Holding Fast to Christ in Sacred Time

1. How has this book reshaped your understanding of Christian observances?
2. What practices, if any, do you now view differently—and why?
3. How can believers disagree on observance without fracturing fellowship?

4. What does it mean to live resurrection-centered lives beyond Easter?
5. How can the church model unity without uniformity in a divided world?

Optional Leader Reflection Questions

- Where might my own convictions be shaping how I judge others?
- Am I teaching history honestly and pastorally?
- Do the practices in my community form Christlike disciples—or merely preserve tradition?
- How can I better shepherd people with differing consciences?

SCRIPTURE INDEX

(Alphabetical by Book; canonical order)

Note: Scripture references are listed as cited or discussed thematically throughout Sacred or Syncretized? Page numbers can be added during final typesetting.

Old Testament

Exodus
- 12:1–14 — Passover instituted; redemptive time and deliverance
- 12:2 — Beginning of months; sacred calendar
- 20:8–11 — Sabbath commandment

Deuteronomy
- 5:12–15 — Sabbath rest and redemption
- 12:29–32 — Warning against syncretism

Psalms
- 105:5 — Remembering God's works
- 119:105 — God's word as guiding light

Daniel
- 12:2 — Resurrection hope within Hebrew theology

Deuterocanonical / Apocryphal (Historical Reference Only)

2 Maccabees
- 12:44–45 — Prayer for the dead (discussed historically, not doctrinally)

Note: Referenced for historical theology discussion only, not as canonical authority.

New Testament

Matthew
- 1:18–25 — Birth of Jesus (Incarnation)
- 2:1–12 — Nativity narrative
- 26:17–30 — Passover context of the Last Supper

Mark
- 14:12–25 — Passover and Last Supper
- 16:1–8 — Resurrection narrative

Luke
- 1:26–38 — Annunciation
- 2:1–20 — Birth of Christ
- 22:14–20 — "Do this in remembrance of Me"

John
- 1:1–14 — The Word made flesh
- 18–19 — Crucifixion during Passover
- 20:1–18 — Resurrection on the first day

Acts
- 2:22–36 — Resurrection-centered preaching
- 4:10–12 — Salvation in Christ alone
- 10:39–43 — Apostolic proclamation of resurrection
- 15:1–29 — Jerusalem Council (practice vs. salvation)
- 17:22–31 — Cultural engagement without syncretism
- 20:7 — Early Christian gathering on the first day

Romans
- 6:1–11 — Resurrection life and discipleship
- 14:1–12 — Liberty of conscience
- 14:5–6 — Disputable days

1 Corinthians
- 5:7 — Christ our Passover
- 8:1–13 — Conscience and liberty
- 10:14–22 — Pagan worship vs. Christian allegiance
- 11:23–26 — Lord's Supper as remembrance

- 15:1–28 — Resurrection as essential gospel truth
- 15:17 — "If Christ has not been raised…"

Galatians

- 4:9–11 — Warning against returning to bondage through days and seasons

Colossians

- 2:16–17 — No judgment regarding festivals or Sabbaths
- 2:20–23 — Human regulations vs. true spirituality

1 Thessalonians

- 4:13–18 — Resurrection hope

1 Timothy

- 2:5 — Christ as the sole mediator

Hebrews

- 4:9–10 — Sabbath rest fulfilled in Christ
- 5:14 — Discernment and maturity
- 11:1–40 — Faithful witnesses
- 12:1–2 — Cloud of witnesses; Christ-centered focus

James

- 1:22 — Obedience, not ritual only

Revelation

- 1:10 — "The Lord's Day"

ABOUT THE AUTHOR

Bishop Antonio M. Palmer is the Senior Pastor of Kingdom Celebration Center and the Presiding Bishop of Kingdom Alliance of Churches International, overseeing a global network of 81 churches. With a ministry rooted in the Gospel since 1993, he planted his first church in Annapolis, Maryland, in 1995 and became a beacon of leadership, service, and transformation.

A passionate advocate for missions, Bishop Palmer leads leadership conferences, plants churches, and provides humanitarian aid to thousands of children in need across the globe. His work includes substantial financial support for orphanages in India and East Africa, demonstrating a steadfast commitment to serving the underserved.

Bishop Palmer, a respected community leader, is celebrated for fostering unity and collaboration among diverse groups. His efforts address critical issues, promote meaningful dialogue, and inspire transformative change. He holds a Bachelor of Divinity, Master's in Pastoral Counseling, and a Doctorate of Divinity. He has been recognized with numerous accolades, including two Governor Citations, two County Executive Citations, Dr. Martin Luther King Jr. Drum Major Award, and the Presidential Lifetime Achievement Award.

As an entrepreneur, Bishop Palmer owns Kingdom Publishing LLC, Antonio Marlin Art, and Kingdom Kare, Inc., a thriving nonprofit organization. He is also the author of ten more impactful books:

- The Irrevocable Covenant
- When We Were Them

- Divine Manifestations: Angels and Theophanies in Biblical Studies
- Rooted and Grounded in Love [Anthology]
- Living By the Spirit
- Love Thyself: Empowering Men for Healthy Living
- God's Rest Revealed: A Life Flowing with Milk and Honey
- Building an Effective Prayer Life
- Mark the Perfect Man: How to Find a Model of Maturity
- Revival: God Will Come Where You Are
- Little Kairo Takes on the World (Children's Book)

To contact the author, please email him at:

Godwillcome2U@gmail.com

www.ingramcontent.com/pod-product-compliance
Lightning Source LLC
Chambersburg PA
CBHW051207120626
46547CB00013B/1234